No Greater Burden

FOR IT SEEMED GOOD TO

THE HOLY GHOST, AND

TO US, TO LAY UPON YOU

NO GREATER BURDEN...

ACTS 15:28

No Greater Burden

A Seeker's Perspective of Anabaptist Culture

Thomas C. Johnson

No Greater Burden

 **Solomon's Press**

© May 2018 Solomon's Press

All rights reserved. No portion of this book may be reproduced by any means, electronic or mechanical, including photocopying, recording, or by any information storage retrieval system, without written permission of the copyright owner. Permission is granted, however, for inclusion of quotations up to 500 words in a non-commercial work, without prior notice. This permission is contingent upon the inclusion of this book title, publisher's name and address with any quotation, and that a copy of the publication in which the quotation appears is sent to the publisher at the address below.

A non-commercial work is any work not intended to be sold for profit. Articles submitted to periodicals for a one-time fee are considered non- commercial.

Most scripture quotations are from the King James Version.

ISBN-13:978-0692074992 (Solomon's Press)
For additional copies contact:

Solomon's Press
Phone: 208-297-0179
Email: solomonspress@gmail.com

Author | Thomas C. Johnson

Contents

Introduction ii
    Why Leave The "Good Life"? iii
    The Seed of Change iv
    What Kind of Life to Live? vii
    Alone or Together? vii
    Which Community? ix
    Discovering the Christian Communities x
    Our Visits xii
    Pressing On xvi
    A Perplexing Irony xviii
Part 1 - Where Are We? 2
    Life Cycles 3
        Conception and Birth 3
        Adoption 4
        Adolescence 5
        Adulthood 6
        Children 8
    A Look Inside 9
        New Terms 10
        Balance Scale 11
        What Is Culture? 11
        What Makes a Culture? 12
        Differences Between Cultures 12
        Responses *to* Newcomers 15
        Responses by Newcomers 16
    Creating an Ethnic Society 21

Effects of Culture upon Church Character	22
Summary	39
Part 2 - How Did We Get Here?	42
Early Church	43
Constantine	44
Dark Ages	45
Reformation	46
American Religious Environment	53
Summary	57
Part 3 - Where Do We Go From Here?	60
A Starting Point	60
The Bible	60
An Example from Early Christianity	63
An Example from the Reformation	68
Refocusing	70
Three Options	71
Renewal	75
A Redeemable Situation	76
Starting New As A Group	77
Summary	87
Conclusion	90
Let's pull this all together	90
Epilogue	96
Appendix 1 - Article XIX	100
Signs of the Church of God	100
First – Saving Faith	100
Second – New Birth	101
Third – Good Works	101

    Fourth – Purity of Heart 101
    Fifth – Faithful Ministers 102
    Sixth – Godly Love 102
    Demonstrating Christianity to the World 102
Appendix 2 - The Servant Leader 108
    Serves a High Calling 108
    Committed to His People 109
    Expects Much 109
    Blazes a Trail 109
    Builds On Strengths 110
    Effective Communicator 110
    Resourceful In Meetings 110
Bibliography 113

No Greater Burden

Introduction

Introduction

The journey of life for the Johnson family was altered with one visit to the Christian Community in Cookeville, Tennessee in March of 1998. Here is how I described our journey leading up to that time in a writing I called *"Discovering the Christian Communities"* ...

Over the previous 6 years, the Lord had been gently but steadfastly leading our family to leave the "good life" and to seek a lifestyle which is more simple and which encourages our godly behavior. During the process of our seeking we discovered the Christian Communities. In 1998 our family made a number of visits to the communities in Cookeville and Decatur Tennessee. Since then we have had numerous requests to hear our impression of these visits. Many wanted to know what they believe and how they live. Others wanted to know why we even visited in the first place and what we were looking for. It's been amazing to us how many people have heard something about the communities, and for reasons ranging from mere curiosity to sincere interest, want to learn all they can about them. Therefore, we felt it would be helpful to ourselves and others to put down in writing our story and explain why we went and what we learned.

No Greater Burden

Why Leave The "Good Life"?

Many ask us why we would want to consider leaving the undeniable "necessities" of life, such as an excellent job with superior benefits and retirement options; the luxury of rural country living; the security of life, home, automobile and health insurance; and all of the conveniences of the modern world such as electricity, internal combustion engines, automobiles, trucks, tractors, telephones, computers, televisions, radios, blenders, microwave ovens, VCRs, musical instruments, electricity and gas ranges, hot water heaters, automatic clothes washers and dryers, vacuum cleaners, air conditioning, hot and cold running water, flush toilets, showers, weed whackers and power tools? And on top of that exchanging it all for a life of hard physical labor, denial of physical pleasures, and a lack of independence. Why? The simple answer is that through a long series of changes in our lives, we came to desire a simpler life, and to share it with others who also want to live a simpler life. Why? While not evil in themselves, we came to recognize the things we wished to give up as conduits and connection points to things which are. We desired instead to include things in our lives which would enable us to be more Christ-like and Christ-dependent. We wanted things in our lives which would not tempt us away from a godly life, but lead us toward it. We also wanted to live with people who thought the same way.

We realized that living in a community of like-minded believers who themselves live simple lives was not the goal in itself. But we thought such a way of life would help us live a more godly life and be more dependent upon God. We knew that any community of people was going to be a community of sinners. But living among sinners saved by Grace and striving for godliness appeared to us to be more spiritually healthy than living among sinners striving to accumulate the riches and the pleasures of this world. We knew we were weak and easily tempted to sin and, stray, so we recognized our

Introduction

need to have people around us who were able to help us be strong and resist temptation. We believed this was the reason God designed the Church, and gave it the authority and structure He did. We sought to be a part of a Church community as much in line with the original design as possible. Thus we sought living in a Christian community with like-minded believers. Such a community is not *the* way, but a better way than many other options we've seen. Is it possible? Did such a community exist? We believed so.

The Seed of Change

In order to understand the changes we experienced, the reader needs to understand what we changed from. Since marrying in 1979, my wife and I had been what most people would consider the typical American couple. I had a good job with the government, we were striving to have a nice home, with many modem conveniences. We were working to have good, reliable cars. We lived in a nice neighborhood in the city. We tried to live a good, clean life. As much as our modem American lifestyle allowed us, we were very involved in our modem American church. Our inbred patriotism also affected much of what we did. Some of you might ask, "What's wrong with that?" I suppose the answer for many could be "nothing." And at the time, we didn't think there was anything wrong with it either, but as time went on, we were compelled to see this differently.

The seed for these changes was planted in 1986 when we made the decision to homeschool our oldest child. Despite the fact that we were fully involved in the modem American pursuit of happiness, we saw a danger in placing our children in the public school system. We are glad we made the decision to school them at home. But real changes didn't begin until 1992 when we became aware that the modem American denominational church system did not seem to be anything like the church described in the New Testament this is a whole different story in itself, but we'll just say that for many reasons, we ended up separating from that system. Being unable to find others of like mind with whom to meet in our local area, we began worshipping the Lord at home, as a family.

As we began reading and studying the Bible without outside influence, we began seeing things we had not seen before. For one, we became convinced that it was necessary for my wife and daughter to wear headship veilings. It was difficult to obey this immediately, so it started out as a small, thin lacy one worn only during worship times, but eventually it became a full covering worn all the time. That brought about many other changes, particularly to our wardrobe, since head coverings didn't seem to go with many of the clothes we had. We never were fancy dressers, but many of our clothes just didn't seem to be appropriate anymore. But we were in somewhat of a quandary as to what exactly we should wear. We came to the conclusion that generally, the clothes anybody wears identifies them with some person, group or trend. With that being the case, we decided we should wear clothes that identified us with people whom we thought lived their lives closer to Biblical teachings. We thought it might be helpful to consider what others have done. This got us to thinking about the Plain people (whom we consider to be Amish, Mennonite, and Brethren). On the surface, we liked what we saw, and began adapting clothing styles from these groups. Not that these styles were sacred, or spiritual, but in our eyes they are characteristic of people who are known to be separate from the world for what we thought are the right reasons.

Along with making changes in our clothing, we began to be convinced through our continued study of the Bible, that there were many other areas in our life that weren't consistent with what we were reading. We began trying to live more simply, with less reliance on convenience items. Not that this was necessarily more spiritual, but it was part of an effort to "unplug" from modern American consumerism. Again, not that consumerism is bad in itself either, but for us we felt it connected us with and made us dependent upon a

Introduction

system that did not support our values. That system also seemed (and still does) to be very unstable and fragile, and we felt uncomfortable allowing our physical well-being to be fully dependent upon it.

When our microwave finally quit working, we didn't replace it. We started buying books to try to learn about being more self-sufficient and to grow more of our own food. We started raising chickens. Eventually we moved to a place where we had more room to try small scale farming. We started raising goats and rabbits. When we purchased that farm, we did get a large tractor. We had a desire to work with horses, and learn how to use them to do work around the farm. We eventually found some. We even got rid of our credit cards, and made an effort to become debt free. Eventually we were. We know that there is no way we can be fully separate from this system, but we felt it should be our goal to depend on it as little as possible.

Along with these lifestyle changes, we also began having new convictions on what our role should be in the political system and its operation. We started seeing the message of Christ as being one of non-resistance of evil. We began to recognize His kingdom as being separate from that of this world and we, likewise, being part of His kingdom were also to be separate from the world. This caused changes in our participation in elections, political activism, and government. We started to feel that my career with the military was not appropriate. We did not consider quitting immediately, since we felt that would be rather foolish and perhaps presumptuous upon God, considering we as a family still needed to eat and pay bills. But we did start planning to quit working for the government long before reaching retirement age.

So in summary, we gradually changed from a life where our lifestyle was dictated by the expectations of modern American society, and where our faith was made to fit into it where possible, to a life where our faith dictated our lifestyle.

What Kind of Life to Live?

At that point, we started to try to put together a good picture of what type of life we wanted to move toward. As I said, we saw the need to live somewhat more simply, and had already begun to experiment with some of those ideas. But we felt we needed to really define just how simply we were going to live. Were we going to keep using electricity and telephones? Did we still want to use things like chainsaws and power mowers and rototillers, or go much further and do things by hand? What kind of house did we want to live in? How were we going to build it? Where should we go? The more we thought about these things, the more we became convinced that the less complexity we were able to have in our lives, the better off we would be in the long run. Granted, it would take some time and learning to get used to living without many of the things we were accustomed to, but we were willing to try.

Alone or Together?

We then tried to decide where we would live after quitting my work with the government. We first thought of finding a very rural piece of property somewhere and building our own "place in the woods" in which to live our simple lives. But we began to realize that not only was my wife's and my future at stake, but our children's as well. What future would they have living on 100 acres off by themselves? And what if we couldn't provide all of the things we needed to live? What if we needed help with something? More importantly, we also became more convinced that being the weak, sinful creatures we were, we needed companionship, accountability and support in our spiritual walk. We found the apostle, Paul's

Introduction

admonition to not forsake the assembling of ourselves together taking on a new light.

So as attractive as living in the woods seemed, we had an increasing desire to share our lives with others of like mind. But again, we were in a predicament we didn't know how to resolve. We felt that the apostle Paul constructed the church in a very simple fashion, and that all of the believers in a given geographical area should "share all things in common". For example, we should be able to expect all Christian believers in our little town to share the same faith, share the material goods that God has entrusted to them as each had need, meet regularly to build up, encourage, edify, and to support each other with the gifts that God has given each one. Instead, what we saw many different "denominations," each with their own "pastor", church building, programs and agenda, all dividing the church into competing segments.

Because of what we considered a "brokenness" in the church, we realized we weren't going to see what we wanted to see, and would probably wait the rest of our lives for like-minded people to move next door. Thus we came to the conclusion that we needed to relocate to a place where others of like mind have purposefully congregated for the same reasons. Thus, we began looking for an intentional Christian community, or in other words, an area where like-minded Christian believers accumulated by design and for the purpose of supporting and encouraging one another in their common goals and beliefs. I have to admit that we had some apprehensions about this, since people living in an intentional community is not the norm in America. Most of the exposure we had to community living was through media stories, and they usually were not good ones. Most examples we thought about were of groups which were quite radical, bizarre or dangerous. Would we be sucked into something that we had always felt was wrong, and had been warned about? We certainly didn't want to be, so we were very cautious. But, we couldn't help thinking that there must be some community living that wasn't radical, bizarre or dangerous. Couldn't it work with good people? Couldn't there be good communities with the right motives and attitudes? We hoped so, and were willing to look for one.

Which Community?

Besides the spiritual values we were looking for in our community, we felt it necessary that it include a lifestyle which was based on the simple lifestyle we had determined to be important. Could we find such a thing? We weren't sure. There must be others who felt the same way we did, we thought. As we would find out, indeed there were.

We looked closer at various Old Order Amish, Mennonite and German Baptist communities. As we learned more about them, there were some things that seemed to closely resemble that of the early church. In fact, as mentioned earlier, we adapted various pieces of their lifestyles into our own. But as to actually joining one of their communities, we found barriers which we were not sure how to overcome.

One barrier for some of these groups was that of language. Many speak (and require members to speak) a form of German, and we didn't speak German. There was also a cultural barrier. Some groups were not receptive to people who come from "non-plain" backgrounds. Others had what we felt were serious doctrinal problems or had lost their original spiritual vitality through many years of following tradition. Therefore, we also looked into other recently formed Christian communities which did not have a "plain" background. There are many out there. They all seemed to have some aspects that were very attractive, but also seemed to have aspects that we couldn't accept.

Introduction

An issue for us at the time was whether or not individual families in the community owned personal property. At that point, we didn't think we could handle a commune arrangement.

Discovering the Christian Communities

We became aware of the Christian Communities when a friend loaned us a stack of various magazines dealing with homesteading, homeschooling, and simple Christian living back in 1996. Included in that stack was a small newsletter from the Christian Communities called the *Update*. It was in a small booklet form and was done entirely by typewriter. We read it, but didn't think much about it at the time, since living in a community was not an interest of ours then. Later, when we did begin taking an interest in community living, we heard again about the Christian Communities through other friends. Each of these people had heard something about them, but weren't sure about their beliefs, practices, location, etc. We began to try to find out something more, but it was difficult.

Early in 1998 a friend of ours had a friend who was visiting them and happened to loan them three back issues of the Update from 1996. We were able to borrow them and make copies to read (the Christian Communities do not copyright their written material). Of course, we then remembered the issue of that little newsletter we had read earlier. From those issues we were able to get a brief glimpse of what this community was like. It helped us make a determination as to whether or not to include them on our list of possible communities and continue investigating them. What we read seemed interesting and didn't contain anything that we couldn't live with. We were attracted to what we could see as a simple, plain lifestyle, but didn't know much else about them. About the same time, we began reading the news reports written by them in a newspaper out of Sugarcreek, OH called the Budget, which carries news reports from many plain groups around the country. We liked what they were writing. The Christian Communities were rising to the top of our list.

We decided to write to the address which was in the back of one of the Updates, to see if we could get some more information. So, in a letter to the Christian Community at Cookeville, Tennessee, we gave a brief background about ourselves, and asked several questions. A short time later we received from Elmo and Elizabeth Stoll a small booklet and some brief answers to our questions. Also included was a short but warm invitation to visit the community in Cookeville. We were encouraged by this invitation to visit in person. Elmo, by the way, was the bishop (overseer) at the community in Cookeville.

Now as I said, they had sent us a booklet. The booklet was entitled "Why We Live Simply" which was compiled from a series of articles which had appeared in various issues of their Update newsletter. It described, as the title says, why they live a simple life. We read it with great interest. But while it did give us a good picture of why they live simply, it did not really answer the questions we had, which focused primarily on how they live simply. But again, finding nothing yet that bothered us, but much that interested us, we decided we needed more information. Since having someone take time from their family life and busy schedule to write to us seemed to be an unreasonable expectation, we began to see the wisdom in Elmo's suggestion that we visit. It would provide us with a good introduction to the community and the people who live there as well as a way to get answers to our questions. So we decided to plan a trip to Cookeville to get these nagging questions answered.

Introduction

Our Visits

At that time we were living on an 85 acre farm and had animals to tend. Since there was no one available to "farm sit" while we all went to Cookeville, we decided that one of the children and I would go and "spy out the land". We corresponded with Elmo and were again encouraged to come and visit, so arrangements were made to go on a weekend in March. A friend of ours from an Amish community near us was also interested in going, so plans were made for him to travel with us as well. It was a blessing to have him with us, as he was tremendously good company and since he had been to the Cookeville community a couple of years earlier, was able to remember and tell us a bit about what the community was like.

It should have taken about 9 hours of steady driving to get there, but since it was raining heavily and we were talking and not paying close attention to our road signs, we missed several of the freeway exits and wound up adding about 3 hours to our trip. We arrived late, it was already dark, and it was raining heavily as well. This made for a somewhat eerie first impression as we entered the community. We had come from a well-lit world into a world of darkness (no streetlights, no house lights, no porch lights, no garage lights, and no barn lights). Only our headlights illuminated the various outbuildings, horse drawn farm implements, miscellaneous stuff laying by the side of the road, and the occasional house. Finally as we slowly drove down the one lane gravel road, we would occasionally catch a glimpse of the yellow orange glow of kerosene lamps in the homes we passed. It kind of reminded me of scenes from travelogues of primitive native villages I'd seen on TV. With our Amish friend's good memory of his past visit, we managed to find Elmo's driveway. Elmo saw our headlights and came out to greet us in the rain with his kerosene lamp lighting his way. We were glad to see him.

No Greater Burden

Because the weekend of our visit to Cookeville happened to be a weekend when Elmo needed to travel to the Decatur, TN community, we were pleased to be able to take him and another man down there for a partial weekend visit. Thus we were able to meet families from both communities. We stayed in Cookeville Friday night. We had a brief tour of the community Saturday morning before leaving for Decatur.

I must say it looked very much different in the daylight. It was unlike anything I'd experienced before. Not that the buildings or anything else in particular was so unusual, but I had never seen so many obvious "do it yourself" projects all in one place, and on such a large scale. It was clear that all the homes, outbuildings, fences, and other improvements to the land were built by the people of the community.

What we saw was not trashy like some areas, but it was not your well-groomed suburban neighborhood or tidy Amish farm community either. It was obvious that all of the stuff we saw was there because they were needed and used often, and perhaps built or stored where they were in somewhat of a hurry. It looked like (and indeed was) lots of very busy life in progress.

We departed Cookeville in the late morning, and arrived in Decatur in the early afternoon on Saturday. The community there, while laid out differently, looked very similar to the community in Cookeville. Again, I couldn't help thinking that this was the do-it-yourselfers heaven. We had an enjoyable visit with several of the families there. We felt a bit awkward at first, being that we were strangers from outside, and that we knew that no one knew we were coming, let alone staying for the night. But they were all very accommodating, gracious, and hospitable and made us feel at home. We were given a walking tour of the community, and were treated to supper. We spent the night and Sunday morning with David Oberholtzer and his family (he's the bishop of the Decatur

Introduction

community), then attended worship services and shared the noon meal with the community members in the meeting house. In the afternoon we were able to talk to several of the men. We then walked around the community and met several other families. We also saw more of the homes and businesses. We then traveled back to Cookeville Sunday afternoon. We had supper, good conversation and singing at another member's home. We spent the night at Elmo's and left the next morning.

This visit gave us the opportunity to visit two of the communities, and get many of our questions answered. We had a good introduction to intentional community living, and were able to get a clearer picture of how we might or might not fit into such a community. One thing that stood out to us was the unique and clever arrangement made to solve the dilemma of how to handle property. They had devised a kind of hybrid arrangement between communal living and private property ownership. They arranged for the community as a whole to own the land and buildings, but families owned their own personal items such as household furnishings and farm implements, and worked at family businesses in the community to supply their own needs. Their sharing with others from the fruits of their own labors as needed seemed to facilitate the Lord's desire for community sharing. The community ownership of land and buildings seemed to free the families from burdensome mortgages. I would have to admit that it was at first hard to swallow the possibility of living in a place without having a title deed to "my" property, but later realized that we were already doing that by renting the farm we were living on at the time. As for the community living arrangement though, we had never before considered such a thing. We never knew such a thing existed! This was going to require some serious consideration.

Finally, while we were there we were able to obtain back issues of almost all of the Update newsletters from as far back as 1991. This provided much interesting reading material. They provided us with a good history of the communities and more detailed descriptions of their major beliefs and practices.

After arriving home and sharing our adventure with the rest of the family, I couldn't help think about how, like the Israelite spies, we had "seen the land, and found it was flowing with milk and honey!" Since we had not discovered anything that would make it impossible to consider such a life for ourselves (although as I said, the land ownership arrangement would take some consideration), we began thinking of how to get the rest of the family down to visit so they could get a mental picture of what it was like. Even though we had most of the back issues of the Updates, which formed a very good history of the communities and a good idea of their beliefs, we felt it was very important to get the entire family down for a visit It's one thing to hear about or read descriptions of something, but quite another to actually experience it yourself.

We had one minor problem, however. That was how to leave the farm for four whole days. This is a big problem when there are 4 horses, 11 goats, 2 dogs, 3 cats and 75 chickens to care for daily. Thankfully, we were in a situation with the animals (which occurs only about once a year) where the feeding and watering could be reduced to once per day, and made simple enough that it would not be an overwhelming burden to accomplish by someone not familiar with such a routine. At the same time a family with which we had become good friends very graciously offered to travel the 20 miles one way to do these chores for us while we made our second trip. With this hurdle overcome, we then wrote to Elmo and made arrangements to visit the community again with the entire family in May.

During the May trip, we were blessed with much better weather, and Elmo did not have to travel to another community, so it was a good weekend to get a good view of the community at Cookeville. We arrived earlier in the day on Friday than our first trip, since we

Introduction

had better weather this time and were able to find the place without getting lost. We spent the afternoon, evening and next morning with Elmo's family. They had also planned the rest of our weekend by having meal and sleeping arrangements already made with various families in the community. How nice! We really appreciated this, since we were able to meet a large percentage of the families there. We were able to hear various viewpoints and obtain much valuable advice with different perspectives. I'm sure it was also a relief for the families in the community as well, since it then wasn't a burden on just one of them to house and feed us for the entire weekend.

On Sunday we joined the community families for worship and noon meal in the meeting house. That afternoon we spent with several other families. Our daughter went with a number of others her age on a trip to a nursing home in nearby Livingston to sing hymns to the residents there. The trip was two hours, one way by horse and wagon (it would have been 20 minutes by car)!

That Monday' we left with sadness because we had made many friends but most importantly, because we had a good feeling that we were welcome there. We came home with much to talk about for weeks.

As God would have it, our visits in March and May were the only visits in which we would have the pleasure of being able to get to know our new friend Elmo Stoll. God called him home suddenly in September 1998 with a massive heart attack.

Pressing On

As a result of what we discovered, our family had become convinced that living in the Christian Communities would meet our desires for a simple, intentional community life, and appeared to be where God was directing us. In addition to this, we felt that an equally important aspect of confirming this as God's will was that the families in the communities have as much peace about us as we did about them. Because of various commitments, making the move wouldn't occur until the summer of 1999. In the meantime, we continued to visit on a regular basis. The impression we received during our visits was that we would be welcome when the time came to actually move. Of course, we realized that there would have to be room in one of the communities for another family when the time came. But, that was out of our hands. Until then, we continued to simplify our lives where we were and to make necessary preparations for an eventual move.

Fast forward one year from then to 1999 and you would find us visiting the Christian Community in Smyrna, Maine because Cookeville simply had no room for one more family. Smyrna was situated on 300+ acres and at the time had only 5 families. After that two week visit we decided to move to Maine.

Introduction

A Perplexing Irony

Now, ironically after 17 years of living in Maine, I find within myself a growing unease. I am asking questions. I probably should have asked some of these questions early on, but didn't think to. At the heart of these it is: Have Old Order churches allowed a "greater burden" to creep in unnoticed? I hope to bring you along as I try to find some answers. I want to look at whether or not the ethnic society that I am enjoying matches the original plan Jesus had for his Kingdom. I am not a theologian, historian, nor a prophet. But I have a few books to read, a little bit of personal experience, and many questions. I don't have the answers, but I've gleaned a few things. On the following pages I hope to peel back the top layer of this experience and take a look inside. I see this as a journey, not only for us and the group we were with, but also Old Order groups, of which our group was a part. This journey affords us the ability to learn and grow. Sometimes that process involves a reassessment of where we are, where we are going, particularly now when the going gets rough and confusing. A careful look at where we are at the moment, determining how we got here, and then deciding where to go next. Let's do that…

Thomas C. Johnson

Smyrna, Maine

2016

No Greater Burden

Where Are We?

Part 1 - Where Are We?

As I sit on our front porch looking out over our green pasture, while our horse peacefully grazes in the afternoon sun, I am reminded of the goodness of God. From here I can see the surrounding hillsides full of blazing fall colors. My wife has joined me with a cup of hot chocolate, and is working on knitting an outfit for a grandchild. I am surrounded by Christian neighbors. What blessings! Many people would wish to be in our shoes. We are not worthy of such blessings. I consider the fact that life is not like this everywhere. I am living in a situation that seems too good to be true. In the Introduction, I gave you a glimpse into our personal history and how we came to make the decision to move to this setting. Now, let's look how the Christian Community in Smyrna Maine turned into an Old Order Amish church...

Life Cycles

When I pondered the history of the Christian Communities, it occurred to me that its development is somewhat like the life cycle of a person; starting with conception, then birth, infancy, childhood, adolescence, adulthood, etc. Unfortunately, for the Christian Communities as a fellowship of churches, death occurred early in the life cycle. Our family arrived on the scene just before its death. We think it was an important part of our lives, though, even as short as it was.

Conception and Birth

The conception of the Christian Communities can be gleaned from Elmo's writing "Let US Reason Together." The birth of Cookeville and the rest of the communities I will leave to someone who experienced that. My modern American mind still marvels at the fact that after visiting Cookeville six times and Smyrna once we were allowed to move in and begin building a homestead. At this point I'm not sure it matters what others were thinking and feeling then, but I believe we probably would not be as quick now to recommend an unproven family make such an investment without more time for observation.

During the first year in Smyrna our family's focus was mostly on building our house. That was also a time of getting to know others in the church and trying to fit in to a new life style. There was much to take in. There were many work bees, helper's and hours spent building our house by hand with no power tools. All this blissfully going on while the Communities were becoming fatally ill. Not being members, we did not hear all the news and didn't understand all the emotions the others were experiencing. We were kept somewhat informed, and were allowed to sit in on some member's meetings, but we were still too new to really grasp it all.

Where Are We?

As I view it, it was in the childhood stage of the life of the Smyrna community that its parents died. What should this little orphan community do to survive? I clearly remember, however, trying to understand why Smyrna would have to break up just because the others did. The church was still made of the same people. We seemed to be getting along OK. Why couldn't we continue? It took a while to realize how that looked to the others in the community. It took longer to realize that even though an orphan may be able to survive on its own, it is-far better to be adopted.

Adoption
And adopted we were, by the Old Order Amish of Michigan. At the time, we were thankful for that adoption. Our family probably will not really be able to grasp all that it took to keep this community alive. This little group did not have any great impact worthy of the effort it took. But as one from the modern American society, I marveled at the effort and dedication shown by many bishops, ministers and brethren to lend help and support to this little group.

But through that experience, Smyrna changed. To us as a family, the conversion to Amish life *was* in some aspects minor, and some major. While the Christian Communities effort was to "reform the plain churches", some of those reforms needed to be surrendered. In some ways life did not change for us. Some changes were easier to adopt. As much as we appreciated and supported the level of technology of the Christian Communities, it was not that hard to step up a notch. The use of motors, phones and battery tools didn't come back that hard. But the most difficult change for us was the use of German in church services. On the positive side, I wouldn't have had the privilege of learning some deep and meaningful German hymns. Nor would have I been able to learn how to sing and appreciate slow tunes. Our brethren and sisters became masterful translators for the sermons. In all this, those from Michigan and some other states helped provide a stability and connection with others of like mind.

Smyrna became an Amish community-with a limp. They wore new clothes, but they didn't fit quite right.

Smyrna's vision of outreach had not changed. It *seems* the heart to welcome those from other cultures continued. But for some years, growth was slow. Survival still was large in our eyes. It was not smooth sailing, but we had a rescue boat to follow.

Adolescence

Adolescence, a new stage of life for Smyrna, came when there was enough growth and stability to ordain new ministry. Growth was slow, but there nonetheless. More seekers were becoming interested, as well as Amish from other states. As growth occurred, we needed new land for homesteads. While Smyrna did have over 300 acres, that did not seem enough considering the types of land it had, and the needs of community. So more land was purchased to accommodate new families. The church adopted an allowance for private property ownership. In those years acquiring needed land and homes became an important effort. It didn't seem like much was available, considering our desire to be close together. The desire to have all live on contiguous properties did not fade much. While we have some brethren who prefer the Amish model of individual farm ownership, all supported the community land ownership model as well. Therefore, Smyrna developed a hybrid approach to land ownership.

During this time of growth Smyrna encountered other issues. Some became lessons learned, some still may need more time and experience to learn. Life even included getting some spankings from our adoptive parents who saw some issues of concern.

Where Are We?

Adulthood

Somewhere in this time period, Smyrna became an "adult" community (maybe "mature" would be a better word). A bishop was ordained. Some of the wrinkles in practice had been ironed out. Smyrna started getting more attention from interested Amish and non-Amish people. But with age comes bigger issues. Smyrna experienced some families choosing to leave (both Amish and non-Amish alike). How humbling. How painful. Why? Who was to blame? That line of thinking usually was not profitable. Some groped for explanations and wanted to know what went wrong. As far as we could tell, no answers presented themselves. But nevertheless, we had to decide how to handle their property. They wanted their money back from what they had put into their homesteads, and in some cases it seemed like they invested more than the church wanted to invest in things they felt were important. That created a very delicate situation! We put together a three man committee to appraise the property and gave them an offer. We wound up paying what they wanted. But it was a lesson to us to be more involved in the house design and building efforts in the future.

When the Community began, it had one tract of land, with the names of several brothers on the deed. There was only one deed for all the different parcels and homesteads. Individual deeds were not issued. But when we agreed to allow private property ownership, new issues arose. One of our properties changed hands three times, resulting in the payment of lawyer fees and transfer taxes three times. To avoid this in the future, we put together a land trust agreement, using trustees to purchase land for the Trust. The church became the beneficiary of the Trust, and when property changed occupants, it did not change ownership. It remained community property, no matter who moved in or out. Private ownership was still an option, but we encouraged putting newly purchased property into the Trust.

Part of adulthood involves managing finances. The church still desired to manage its finances as a brotherhood, making money available to the brothers for purchasing land, businesses, and buildings from within the community. We encouraged lending to one another as needed, with no interest charged. This was done either privately if possible, or from the Community Fund. The Community Fund was managed by a Finance Committee, made up of the Deacon and two brothers selected by the church. Money put into the Fund could either be donated or loaned to it. All the money in the Fund was there on a free will basis. At that time there was no mandatory contributions. This worked fairly well. To help all of us be on the same page regarding the financial policies of the church, the ministry developed several sets of "guidelines", covering the Finance Committee, Community Fund, businesses and finances in general.

Having finances to manage meant that most of the families had some way of producing income. At that stage of community adulthood, with 21 families, there were at least a dozen businesses, a dairy or two, several produce farms and several small home businesses providing income. To make sure all have gainful employment takes some effort and sacrifice. Not all were farmers, obviously, even though the emphasis was on agricultural work. As others have stated, a church which is "seeker oriented" soon faces certain issues. Those not used to providing incomes by using their hands found it hard to supply the needs of their families with the work available. The lack of work ethics, at times, was an issue.

I don't know how it is in other states, but businesses in Maine have to pay income taxes, Social Security tax, Unemployment tax, as well as provide Workman's Compensation insurance. This issue could be an interesting topic of discussion. A clear answer for these issues was not readily available. How should Christians view the taxes of the land? Should Christian employers collect social security taxes for their employees? Are there taxes that should be ignored and taxes that should be paid? Should workers be paid just cash? Should all income be reported? Questions like these floated around. What about hiring a non-member seeker? A seeker interested in becoming a part of the church sometimes needed an income in order to stay long enough to evaluate things. We developed an agreement to hire seekers on a temporary basis, collecting the required taxes and paying them. We also came up with a paper for them to sign stating that they understand that they are being hired on a temporary basis while they evaluate the church for possible membership. We also ask them to agree to take responsibility for any injury or loss they may experience. Working for us was at their own risk.

Regarding Workman's Compensation, Smyrna took the stand that since we do not use insurance or government aid, and we accept all personal risk we refrain from buying Workman's Comp policies for our workers. Sometimes we are asked how we can justify this when other businesses in the state must do it, and it gives us an unfair advantage. We justified it with the thought that we did not expect to be compensated by others for our losses. Those who live and work in society at large have come to expect this. That expectation resulted in laws being enacted to require the employer to buy insurance for them. That choice is an expensive one and it is what created an economic disadvantage for them. Right or wrong, we chose to exclude ourselves from that approach.

Children
With the passage of time my wife and I had the privilege of seeing two of our three children get married and establish their own households. Others have as well. Many children living in the community eventually grew up and started their own families. Others continued to move in. This growth motivated Smyrna to define some things more clearly. How big should the church be? How many families? We eventually decided to have a total of 25 homesteads. There were a few small cabins as well. The number of families living in the community fluctuates around that number.

From the beginning, Smyrna had a vision of starting other churches when it was able. Like our own children having children of their own, the church came to the point where it had the resources and courage to reproduce itself. When it began the effort to start an outreach, the vision was to have a large community-owned tract of land all contiguous and connecting. We were fortunate to find 3 large tracts to buy, all next to one another. We formed a land trust to purchase those tracts. That land was large enough to support about 12 families. One lesson learned through that situation, was that it's important to divide the large tracts into parcels before anyone gets attached to "their" spot. We were a bit late in that resulting in extra work to get things adjusted.

In that outreach effort, the church selected two minister families to send. Then they selected 10 more families to be placed in a pool of names. From that pool the ministry selected five families to go. Those who owned homesteads in Smyrna sold them to the Land Trust. The amount they received was determined by the Finance Committee.

With two of our three children married, the "empty nest" situation was coming upon us. What to do? Not all children are prepared or able to build "dawdy houses" for their parents. The children and the parents may not be ready for that. With a vision of maintaining small communities, this was an unlikely solution. We didn't think about *that* when we moved in. Life has a way of taking unforeseen turns, and usually in far less time than expected. And so it took us for a turn as well.

A Look Inside

Now that you have a glimpse of the journey we have taken, and an idea of the growth and early changes that happened in the church, let's peel the top layer off and get a look inside. How did all this work, and what are some of the more subtle effects of an Old Order way of

Where Are We?

life? In all of our minds I believe there was a serious desire to live life according to our understanding of what the Bible teaches. This effort produced both positive and negative results. But the process was difficult. It required much diligence and perseverance. For us who weren't raised in this type of setting, it required much change.

New Terms

One change for us started with terms. One of these, of course, is ***Anabaptist.*** Others followed. When we first came to this church, we were introduced to the term *seeker.* Seekers are people who come to an Anabaptist church from a non-Anabaptist background. So when we came here, we became "seekers". I think of it as a convenient label for those of us who have an identity different from that of the Anabaptists.

Another term was ***Plain.*** We refer to this often. Who are Plain People? This has been a puzzle to me and increasingly so over the years. Initially, I had ideas about this when moving to Maine, but have come to realize they were loaded with assumptions that have proven false. I have not really heard a clear definition. I don't think Webster's will help us here. It seems to be a broad term, and there doesn't seem to be much agreement even in plain circles. I use the term loosely here to refer to "conservative Anabaptists", realizing that the term "conservative" is also relative. Perhaps it could also refer to groups who in some way have defined their own culture.

In this writing, ***Dynamics*** is a term I will use. It is a small word which says much. In this discussion, I use it to mean a process of growth, change, or interaction.

Assumptions and expectations are two more words you will see. I view these as parts of an attitude we have toward the unknown before we have the facts. It is closely tied to our experience and imagination. It's a way we have to "fill in the blanks" since we don't usually like blanks.

Balance Scale

In discussions about seekers, generally the context is whether or not they make it. Failure seems to be synonymous with seeker. Few are successful. Successful at what? I suppose it should suffice to say that if a seeker leaves before he dies, his effort to join the plain people is not successful. From a seeker perspective this may seem like just one more step in the journey. But from an Old Order perspective to leave an Old Order setting can seem more like losing the faith entirely.

I like to make use of the concept of a balance scale. On one side of the scale are the things that are given up to join (losses). On the other side are things which are perceived to be better (gains). This scale, I believe is mostly unconscious. It becomes conscious when too much trouble arises. There seems to be a threshold of tolerance which when surpassed, brings the idea of leaving to mind. That threshold point is not a friend to the seeker. He tries to resist it, but it can become fairly strong. That seems to be when the balance scale is most apparent.

What Is Culture?

In trying to understand the seeker situation, it is important to understand what we mean when we talk about culture. Within the broader Anabaptist circles, there are a variety of subcultures. These play powerful roles in lives at the social level.

Relative to what we are talking about, Webster's dictionary defines culture this way...

> b: **the customary beliefs, social forms, and material traits of a racial, religious, or social group; also: the characteristic features of everyday existence (as diversions or a way of life) shared by people in a place or time.**

Where Are We?

c: the set of shared attitudes, values, goals, and practices that characterizes an institution or organization

All of us have a "native culture", which I would define as the culture in which we were born and raised. Out of that native culture develops expectations and assumptions.

What Makes a Culture?

The bible gives us many commandments. In the New Testament there are over 900...if one considers everything commanded by Jesus and the Apostles. These commandments, in the form of action verbs such as *be, let, let not, make, give, pray, love, take, do, do not, deny, go, teach, endure, render, forgive, obey, submit, ask, repent, seek, keep, rejoice, distribute, pursue, flee, watch, sit, walk, stand, put on, put off,* form principles which define the Christian life. They guide our thoughts, speech and actions, but they do not specifically define how to fulfill them.

It is a natural thing to be frustrated with scripture for not defining clearly how to do things, such dressing modestly. What exactly is modest dress? These are called applications. We know it is necessary at some point to decide how to apply biblical principles. In order for a woman to cover her head, some decision needs to be made as to how to construct the covering and how to wear it. Is this left up to personal liberty, or is it to be defined by the Church? Should everyone's covering in a Church look alike? Should that covering identify which Church a woman belongs to? The answers to these questions determine the type of culture within any Christian group.

Differences between Cultures

I have heard much about Christian culture, American culture, worldly culture, Amish culture, etc. It is easy to paint some as totally bankrupt, evil and wicked. Others are considered totally good and right. I think this is unwise. Is Amish culture completely free of evil? As I have become involved in Amish culture over the years, I have come to realize that the picture is not as pretty as I once imagined. Is

American culture completely wicked? As I review my experience of American culture, I also realize it is not as demon filled as I once thought. Is there a good culture or a bad culture? There are good and bad things in all cultures. But, should I judge another culture as bad? If I do, usually it's the one I'm not in. The point is that we should be slow to judge other cultures. But lest I be misunderstood, let me quickly add that there are practices, values and customs which are healthier than others, considering what God says are healthy, in almost any culture.

Cultural differences, I believe, played a role in the demise of the Christian Communities. The following are some observations of one of its leaders:

> *"Early this spring (2000), the ministry...met to discuss the future direction of the communities and to consider deep concerns about our identity. With courage lagging...it seemed necessary to find out just how each minister felt about the future of the group, and whether it was wise to continue 'forging ahead' with our own unique identity. Each one bared his heart as to his hopes and fears about the future. It immediately became apparent that there were several doubts about the wisdom of continuing on together, from several perspectives. Our renewed appreciation and desire for the traditions of our fathers was bringing us ever closer to an inevitable conflict. There was considerable feeling that the forces and vision that started the communities were flawed, in that they were too critical of the Anabaptist traditions."*

> *"Returning to cherished traditions was proving to be a divisive thing, splitting the members back into the various groups they had come from."*

Where Are We?

> *"Increasingly, people were asking, 'If I am returning to traditions, why should I not accept the ones I'm most comfortable with?'"*

> *"The defense of tradition in intellectual and rational ways could only bring the group toward more conflict as those traditions were defended."*[1]

I believe this is a good example of the impact that culture (stated as tradition) has on church relationships. In this example we see how it impacted the interaction within and the eventual fate of that fellowship of churches. Several things seem to stand out to me in this example. One is the appreciation and desire for the traditions of their youth. No doubt all of them were godly men with strong convictions of their own, but they valued the culture of their youthful days. I believe that each of them, despite their own heritage and traditions still held mutual respect for each other because of their love for Jesus Christ. That is not in question here. In spite of that, their cultural balance scale was eventually tipped back in the favor of the old culture. In the beginning each of them likely left things that they valued in order to become part of the effort with hopes of gain. But with "courage lagging" the old ways again became of greater value. Another point I observed is that even within three Anabaptist groups involved in this effort (Amish, Mennonite and German Baptist), all holding the same core doctrinal beliefs, they viewed various aspects of the same Gospel differently. Can you see the importance of culture here? The defense of these traditions was causing division. The group was becoming polarized along cultural lines (how to do things), and not foundational lines (what to do).

A final item to note in this example is the idea of comfort. The thought that "if traditions must be followed, then why not follow the

---

[1] Geiser, Bryce. 2000. *A Closing Chapter For The Christian Communities*. Old Order Notes.

comfortable ones?" became strong. After years of tiring conflict over tradition and other issues, a comfortable, understandable and familiar culture looked attractive.

We should not ignore culture in our lives, even in our lives of faith in brotherhood. It is part of each of us, and applies to the seeker issue directly. The cultural dynamic of human life is woven through all other dynamics. The influence it has on us can be overridden for a time, much like holding your breath. In the end, however, we will need to start breathing again, either voluntarily or after passing out. Seekers make a conscious decision to override their native culture to forge a new identity with the Plain People. This is similar to the German Baptists, Amish and Mennonites overriding theirs for a time to forge a unique identity together in the above example. In both cases, the ones who put aside their native culture will have courage to continue as long as there is still a perceived gain. Once that erodes, the balance scale tips past center in the direction of loss. Native culture again rises in importance. I do not want to be guilty of ignoring the fact that there may be other factors in all this. I am emphasizing the role culture plays, but other things such as emotional, spiritual and behavioral problems can be involved and complicate the matter.

Generally, what I observed is that mixed religious cultures will work together for a while, but eventually the balance scale tips over unless great effort is made to override the effects. This principle is somewhat like shaking up Italian dressing. If we don't keep shaking, the contents will eventually separate.

Responses *to* Newcomers
In some settings seekers are given responsibility in the church at a lay-person (non-spiritual) level such as on a school board or a finance committee. This could be an indication of a measure of acceptance and trust. I acknowledge a person's individual

capabilities, aptitudes and attitudes will also affect this. A seeker is not entitled to positions of responsibility any more than a member with a plain background. But neither should their opportunities be less because they are not. Scripture seems to tell us that we are all equal in Christ "...for ye are all one in Christ Jesus." (Gal 3:28b). But if we look at the role culture plays in religious group dynamics, we see something else. Human nature is a factor in why an "outsider" from a different culture will be a minority that may be treated differently. I don't think it can be avoided. Right from the beginning the seeker should acknowledge his secondary position in the setting he is joining. If he does not, he may be prone to adopting various false expectations. These expectations, when not realized, can weaken his ability to weather the storms he encounters. Over time, this can tend to walk him to the exit door.

Responses *by* Newcomers

Seekers move to Old Order settings because of anticipated gain. They exchange things in their lives for other things they think are of greater value. When we moved to Maine, we exchanged things in our lives that we were used to for other things that we felt were lacking. We did not know if that exchange would actually provide what we had expected, but we had hope. Some people give up more than others in this kind of exchange. But in order to go through all the pain and effort, there needs to be a hope of gain. I define gain as a perceived improvement in one's walk with Christ. This gain should come from being in a setting which allows a person the opportunity to grow into Christian maturity, and contribute to the growth of Jesus' Kingdom. The effort expended to change cultures needs to result in this gain. Evaluating this is difficult. It is highly subjective. But all take a risk to obtain it.

Tipping the Scale

Seekers make great sacrifices with little information. Some are more thorough in their research about plain people than others. But what they need to know is hard to obtain by outside research. Much is riding on how they fill in the blanks of their knowledge with their imagination. And their imagination is directed by their native culture. What happens, though, when reality hits? What happens when expectations are not met and the imaginations prove false? My observation is that in time the scale on which the seeker is measuring his gain tips the other way toward loss. Eventually the loss side outweighs the gain side. Many seekers who have left these settings have faced this balancing act. Some may have courage to try another one, but usually with less resolve than they had the first time. When they try again, it doesn't take as much to tip the scale again to the loss side. Eventually, they return to their original setting. Some may retain some of their original convictions, some may not. I have witnessed several seekers completely reject Christ after their troubled journey through these settings. My theory is that much of their disillusionment is from false expectations and assumptions concerning the cultural differences they encounter. What kinds of things get placed on the balance scale? I see four categories...

Doctrine

These are the core beliefs and principles which define the foundation of faith and practice.

Function

These are the ways the doctrine is practically worked out. They include ways the church operates and how ministry manages the affairs of the church. This includes such things as the how the meetings of the church are conducted, the school, communion, singings, church discipline, interaction with other churches and those outside the church.

Where Are We?

Relationships
   These are the interpersonal relationships within each family and between brothers and sisters in the church

Form
   These are the things which govern the lifestyle, how we conduct our temporal lives. These include things such as the technology level used, clothing styles, means of communication and transportation, etc. In churches where these things are defined by the church, then they will have a heavier impact on the balance of the scale.

Of these four items, I see the last three defining the culture of the group. They all are important to the seeker as he is involved in the church. It's likely they all do not carry the same weight and may change in their ranking over time.

Most discussions about seekers involve the thoughts and beliefs in their Christian walk. We talk about the differences between various Anabaptist practices as specific applications of biblical principles. If German Baptists, Mennonites and Amish believers are together talking, they can generally agree on basic biblical principles, and be fairly comfortable with each other to a point. But, when they begin to face defining particular applications of these agreed-upon principles, they begin to diverge.

This practice of defining the *applications* of principles as a church is what makes a culture...religious culture. But I couldn't avoid considering the idea that if the church was intended to define them, why are there no hints of it in scripture? Paul addressed many specific problems in the Corinthian church. It was a Gentile Christian church, and had many of the same problems we face today. But he did not address issues beyond the level of principles. Why not?

If we look at the early Christian writings, it is hard to find much discussion about this either. Actually, there are writings that seem to indicate the opposite. (I'll talk more about this later.) There doesn't seem to be any example of (or requirement for) taking the principles and defining them for the whole congregation. The writings of the early Christians, early Anabaptists, van Braght, Menno Simons, Dirk Philips and others seem to have the same silence on the subject. There seems to be no discussion of the responsibility of the church to define a uniquely physical public identity. When I consider the importance placed on this by Old Order groups, I expect to find considerable discussion about it in the scriptures and other significant writings. But these sources seem to be silent.

Some would understand the principle of "being of one mind" to include the idea of unity of practice. Is this what Jesus had in mind? How can we determine this one way or another? On one hand, opposing this could reveal a desire for worldly things. On the other, it appears legalistic. How can we know for sure? Is it simply a matter of choice, and we hope God will bless our choice?

This is where accurate interpretation of scripture is important. How to interpret scripture is a wide topic, and is the cause of much difficulty in the church. The Catholic Church, the Protestants and the modern Anabaptists have run into difficulty because they have used what some call a principle of accommodation. Using this principle allows churches to modify biblical teachings to fit the existing traditions. Church leaders interpret scriptures through the lenses of their situations, deeply rooted culture, history, and preferences. This is evident when we place the establishment of the Anabaptist movement as the "starting point" (or basis) of our biblical interpretation and applications. This becomes a platform on which to build doctrine, and we are in effect raising it above the foundation of

Where Are We?

the Apostles. Isn't this a dangerous platform upon which to stand? A platform is like a foundation. Paul tells us *"For no other foundation can anyone lay than that which is laid, which is Jesus Christ."* (1 Cor. 3:11). What we build on this foundation is also important. Tradition, as the foundation, becomes the predominant influence for the interpretation of right and wrong. The teachings of the forefathers and the centuries of enforcing them forms the substance of truth. It becomes the lens through which scripture is interpreted. This concept is central to what the Anabaptist founders rejected in the Catholic Church.

Getting back to the thought that "being of one mind" would imply unity of practice, then, it seems the principle of accommodation is at work here. When the tradition of uniformity of appearance and methods is my starting point, I'm tempted to interpret scripture with it. It's hard not to allow preconceived ideas influence our interpretations of scripture. It's important, therefore, to take scripture in context and as a whole to make an accurate assessment.

Many times, seekers come from some form of Christian setting. They likely may have been raised with some religious background. As a result of that background they have certain values, customs and practices. Some of these seekers come with a religious background that did not distinguish itself culturally from the surrounding American culture. But they came with a culture nonetheless...a culture that is familiar and understandable. The plain people have in a larger way defined their own social culture as a part of their religious culture. This is often quite different from the greater American culture. It's part of what both attracts and bewilders seekers. In many cases it is their undoing. But the point here is that with a church defined application of biblical principles, culture becomes involved.

Solomon observed a truth about the operation of culture. He wrote "Train up a child in the way he should go, and when he is old he will not depart from it." (Pro 22:6). We think of this often when considering child training, and usually think of it in a moral sense. But I believe it goes deeper. Biblical principles and their applications form a part of our culture. Non-religious practices, customs and traditions also do. They define who we are and how we think from childhood. That is why they are so important to consider and understand when seekers want to join the plain people.

Creating an Ethnic Society

I couldn't help noticing another interesting thing. After several generations of enforcing a culture, a religious ethnic society is produced. It occurred to me that ethnic societies are manmade, sometimes by accident, sometimes on purpose. I looked up the definition of "ethnic" and "society":

> Ethnic: "**Of or relating to large groups of people classed according to common racial, national, tribal, religious, linguistic, or cultural origin or background.**"

> Society: "**A voluntary association of individuals of common ends especially an organized group working together or periodically meeting because of common interests, beliefs or profession; an enduring and cooperating social group whose members have developed organized patterns of relationships through interaction with one another; a community, nation, or broad grouping of people having common traditions, institutions, and collective activities and interests.**"

Defining culture and enforcing it for generations results in an ethnic society. The Old Order groups have done such a thorough job of defining and enforcing applications of bible principles for so long, a well-defined culture has formed. It grew broad and deep. It became exclusive, safe and comfortable for those inside, and unapproachable by those outside. It also created barriers between the church and society. These types of barriers are not the same as the separation spoken of in scripture. They are self-protective.

Let me summarize the main points I've covered so far.

- Culture plays an important part in the dynamics of seeker/plain people relationships. Minimizing that importance on either side can result in difficulties.

- Culture is an unchangeable part of each person's life. It is part of that person's upbringing as Solomon observed. Each person can change how they act and respond to their upbringing, but that isn't easy.

- Culture in Old Order churches is created when they define applications of principles. To try to preserve a culture for generations can be successful in and of itself, but at the expense of spiritual vitality. This is not unlike locking the steering wheel of a vehicle traveling down the interstate. Things may look good and go well for a while, but without adaptation and correction it will eventually run off the road.

- Church culture practiced over generations produces an ethnic society.

Effects of Culture upon Church Character

When a church defines applications for itself, both intended and unintended things result. The character of the church is affected in various ways. Following are some of those ways.

Vision

A vision of a church is like a mission statement. It is not always written, but should be well understood by the whole church. It defines the purpose, thrust and mission of the group. Like standards, a vision should not be assumed. It should be discussed and well known. But when a culture develops over generations, the vision changes. In order to accomplish our best in life, we benefit from clear vision. How well we see also depends on what we focus on. This applies figuratively to this discussion. The things upon which we focus affects the direction we go. The change of focus has occurred in several areas:

- ❖ More on why we do what we do, less on how to do what we should.
- ❖ More on outward things, less on inward.
- ❖ More on applications, less on principles.
- ❖ More on being, less on doing.
- ❖ More on milk, less on meat.
- ❖ More on culture, less on service.

Kingdom

A focus on the culture can produce a distortion of what the Kingdom of God is. We tend to forget some important aspects of it. *"...for the Kingdom of God is not food and drink, but righteousness and peace and joy in the Holy Spirit. For he who serves Christ in these things is acceptable to God and approved by men."* (Rom 14:17). *"For the kingdom of God is not in word but in power."* (1 Cor. 4:20). *"...He answered them and said, 'The kingdom of God does not come with observation;' 'nor will they say, 'See here!' or 'See there!" For indeed, the kingdom of God is within you.'"* (Luke 17:20, 21). The emphasis on preserving the culture takes precedence over preserving the Kingdom. The culture is confused with the Kingdom. A belief that culture facilitates the means of salvation becomes accepted. Any threat to the culture is perceived as a threat to the faith. Acculturation (losing the culture) is equated to apostasy.

Where Are We?

Standards

This is tied directly to the issue of culture. The church exchanges standards based on biblical principles for standards based on applications. As I discussed earlier, this creates a culture. The culture then determines how the standards are written in order to preserve itself. The goal of the standards is to "make application" of biblical principles as the leadership understands them and what they think is best for the church. These applications are well defined and protected by the use of the ban and shunning. They are "extra-biblical" in that they are not specifically prescribed in scripture. There are principles that may support some of them, but these cultural standards usually are highly specific. They define colors, sizes, types, styles, methods, etc. The standards define the culture, and the culture preserves the standards.

Unity

A sure way to produce difficult relationships is to require lock-step uniformity. We can see from Anabaptist history that uniformity of appearance and practices has not produced unity. Instead, it produces division and strife, both within and between churches. Attempting to achieve uniformity of things that were not intended to be uniform produces discord. The degree of discord produced is proportional to the degree to which this is required. The irony is that this pursuit of uniformity results in disunity among brethren who would otherwise be unified. In Romans 14, Paul seems to be trying to remind us that we are not all alike, and there may be diversity in the church. *"Receive one who is weak in the faith, but not to disputes over doubtful things."* (Rom 14:1). *"Who are you to judge another's servant? To his own master he stands or falls."* (Rom 14:4). Also, God reminded Samuel how he looked at outward things... *"But the Lord said to Samuel, 'Do not look at his appearance or at the height of his stature, because I have refused him. For the Lord does not see as man sees; for man looks at the outward appearance, but the Lord looks at the heart."* (1 Sam 16:7). Wouldn't we want to remember this as we try to be united?

Exclusiveness

I shared with you earlier about the difficulties seekers have in joining a new culture. It is difficult enough to have the courage to try to learn to be a disciple of Jesus. Another layer of difficulty is added with the cultural adjustments to make. The barrier culture creates is a two-edged sword. It protects and comforts those inside, but hinders and complicates life for those outside wanting in. Churches which are less focused on outreach benefit the most from this approach. This is a natural characteristic of a monastic view of church life. It is intended to be protective for the ones in the group. The intention, consciously or unconsciously, is to live *out of* the world. Often, when people leave Old Order settings, they are said to have gone back *into* the world. But where did Jesus say we are to be? Paul said we are to *"shine as lights in the world"* (Phl 2:15). So where should we live, in the world, or out of it?

Outreach

Whether one calls this evangelism, missions, the Great Commission, or outreach, the idea is the same. It refers to spreading the news of the Kingdom. Old Orders have generally seemed to accept the view that spreading the gospel involves the following thoughts:

> *"Christ's final commission was fulfilled by the apostles."*

> *"We believe our most effective witness to outsiders is in the way we live, raising families, and quietly earning our bread in the sweat of our faces."*

> *"We must always be ready to give an answer to someone who asks about our faith."*

Where Are We?

> "The reason we don't actively evangelize is because we are nonresistant."
>
> "Outreach is not in harmony with our emphasis on humility."
>
> "It will never work to proselytize outsiders to our way of life; our cultures are too different."
>
> "Our churches would never be able to adapt into foreign cultures. It is a threat to our values and lifestyle."
>
> "The higher Mennonites emphasize outreach, and look where they are now!"
>
> "The scriptures do not command us that we must engage in outreach to be saved." [2]

As a result of these ways of thinking, we have lost heart for an early Anabaptist understanding of outreach. It is something foreign to Old Order theology. A few churches have a vision for planting churches for the purpose of being quiet living examples to American Society. Some have openness to having seekers join them. Some individuals within these setting may personally be quite evangelistic on their own. This is tolerated in some churches. But as a whole Old Order churches do not seem to view it to be a necessary part of church vision.

---

[2] Joshua Zimmerman, *The Missing Spoke*, Old Order Amish Literature Fund, (2017), 19

Body Life

Coupled with the loss of evangelistic zeal is the loss of what I call "body life". I define body life as the work of preaching, teaching, exhorting, admonishing, rebuking, edifying and equipping. These are the ingredients needed for making disciples, equipping them for the work of ministry, interacting as a church, caring for hurting members, restoring errant members to the faith, having small group ministries, and one-anothering. The key to making this work is what we could call *companionship* or *discipleship*.

Communication

Communication is another area affected. This is related closely to body life. If communication suffers between members, the body life is weakened. In some settings, much is expected to be learned by observation. Despite the teaching against gossip, much church news is communicated through the "grapevine" (unofficial talk among some in the group). The ones who don't get around as much don't get as much news. Even important news of meetings and other events, happenings with church members, and needs are often left to be circulated by chance word of mouth. This generally works in a closed society expecting it. But when cross-cultural seekers enter the picture, it can be quite difficult.

Another aspect of the communication difficulties within Old Order Amish and Mennonite societies is the use of the German and Pennsylvania Dutch languages. Within groups which desire to have separation from surrounding society, this provides a formidable barrier and is viewed positively in those settings. For those groups desiring to have some form of witness to that society, the traditional languages have become a bit of a quandary. They make up a sizeable part of the Old Order culture, and can be an additional hindrance to outreach and inreach. The topic of language in Old Order settings is not a new one, and has been well covered elsewhere. My observation is that even with the best of intentions to not make it an issue within

Where Are We?

Old Order settings, it still is. I do not think it is the primary issue, but a significant one.

Family

Most Old Order churches function as a group of families united within the farm based societal framework that defines them. The strong family oriented structure places the body life and care responsibilities I mentioned earlier predominately on the parents. I do not wish to imply taking any of these responsibilities away from them. But it shouldn't be an either/or situation between the church and family. Parents need to be equipped to be good parents. That should be the church's responsibility. Since more than the obligatory meetings of church, school meetings, weddings, baptisms, funerals and the occasional disciplinary members' meeting are thought to interfere with and damage family life, church meetings are held to a minimum. While we emphasize a horse and buggy life style, said to enhance community interaction, there is resistance to "excessive" church functions.

Converts

If a church revives some sort of vision for outreach it faces a dilemma. If someone responds to the outreach, the cultural structure of the church hinders the absorption of that person into the group. In a sense, there is a clash between the generations-old cultural exclusiveness, and the biblically mandated openness. As a result, the church is poorly equipped to disciple a new person into the church. Much is left to be learned by observation. And when the church is largely culture based, a new foreign culture is a large obstacle to learning about following Christ. Most groups do not have an organized way of instructing new interested people in the Christian faith. Unless someone in the congregation takes it upon themselves to teach the basics, that person is left to his observational powers to grasp them.

Help

The difficulties of life affect us all, some more than others. When someone becomes loaded down with burdens too heavy to bear, or becomes overtaken in a trespass, the brotherhood needs to be there to help. For the most part, we have let this part of body life seriously atrophy. I see a growing number of counseling centers, demonstrating the growing need. On one hand I hear statements similar to the advice given by Job's friends; *"Why do we need counseling centers, or even counseling? If a person would just listen to the ministers and submit to the standards, be humble and content, they would not be have problems. It's their own fault."* This is stated a bit simply to make the point. On the other hand I see a growing number of people seeking help from Psychiatrists and Psychologists (modern day philosophy and empty deceit - Col 2:8). A recent article in a popular Old Order publication[3] illustrates the growing trust in this area of "medicine" among the Plain People. To be fair, some groups do try to help the hurting. But they are so committed to cultural preservation, that their ability to help the hurting within the church is severely limited. Teaching one another how to help one another is not considered acceptable. A few Old Order groups try to educate themselves in some form of counseling, but often wind up using an integrated (mixing Psychology and Theology) flavor.

An irony I see here is that the strong motivation for separation that exists in the Old Order circles has crippled their use of biblical materials that could help in this area. The reluctance to receive training seems to make them vulnerable to the very philosophies of the world that they are trying to keep out. Psychology is being mixed with Christianity and since that appears to be a plausible and non-threatening area of science, it is being drawn in. But it must also be said that this practice is not limited to Plain People. It is widespread in Christianity today. But the main point here is that the extra

---

[3] *"Understanding Depression"*, Aylmer, Ontario, Canada, Family Life, August - September 2016

measures of the Old Order groups to remain out of the world and separate from it has not prevented the same thing happening to them. The history, development, and use of Psychology is another topic. But I feel it necessary to point out that it is a far larger threat to Christianity than first appears.[4]

Associations

A common practice in Old Order churches is to prohibit members of the church from interacting with other churches not considered to be in their fellowship. This is an expression of separation. Any interaction (which includes exchanging preachers), with other churches must only be with other specifically identified Old Order groups. Other Anabaptist groups which apply the same biblical principles differently are off limits.

We see an illustration of how God views this in two accounts in Acts. In Acts 10, Peter told Cornelius it had been unlawful for Jews to keep company with or go to one of another nation. But God showed him that he should not call any man common or unclean. The implication here is that not keeping company with or not going to someone is the same as calling them unclean or common (not special as God's people are). But Peter learned that he was not to reject the Children of God just because they were not Jews. Peter made it clear to Cornelius' family that whoever fears God and works righteousness is accepted by God. This relates directly to our situation. We are not to call other Christians unclean just because they are not of our society. Without making a dogmatic point about it, God said the conditions for acceptance is having a fear of God, and working righteousness. Should we demand more?

---

[4] Johnson, Thomas C. *Solomon's Guide To Worship Disorders*, Smyrna, ME: Solomon's Press, 2016

No Greater Burden

Another example of ethnic separation here is shown in the circumcision debate in Acts 15. God's will to include Gentiles in salvation was made clear to a number of the Apostles. Paul said God's will to save Gentiles was predestined. But, the Jews thought in terms of their ethnic society, so they naturally extended the custom of circumcision to the Gentiles. They connected salvation to it. Paul and Barnabas knew otherwise, and contested it. They personally had seen the opposite being accomplished. Peter recognized the reason for this. He saw the cultural requirement as testing God, and being an unnecessary yoke. James defined a key principle: Cultural yokes are not meant to be part of the kingdom. He decided to place "no greater burden" on the Gentiles than was necessary.

Leadership

The purpose and function of the leadership roles are also affected. Instead of leadership being shepherding, it has become hierarchical. Consider the following...

> *"Under the Old Order system the ministers and especially the bishops, often have absolute rule. The system is designed so that the ministry controls all facets of the church service. This includes nearly all planning and definitely all announcements. The layman does nothing at a church service except to usher and lead the singing. The Amish do not intend to make any changes. The fact that very few changes take place among them is due to the way their religious system works. The ministers take their responsibilities very seriously. Decisions on current questions are generally reached by giving the most consideration to possible long term effects. Thus, the present peace and satisfaction of the brotherhood is ignored. In most Amish communities no single congregation can discuss a matter of any magnitude and make their own decision. Questions concerning changing dress standards or things*

of this type are seldom discussed with the brotherhood, except in very rare cases. The congregation is simply asked to agree with the minister's decision. By the time the issue is presented to the church there is only one way to vote, that is in favor of the ministers' motion (forschlage). The motion is usually presented to the congregation by the bishop, and if one doesn't vote in favor of it, he is marked for his lack of cooperation...The above points contribute to building a religious body but are not conducive to spiritual growth within that body." [5]

Even in settings where the leadership is concerned about spiritual wellness, this is the approach. The culture needs to be protected in order for it to survive. A leadership style that involves the brotherhood in the decision making process threatens the survival of culture. Much more control is required to achieve long term consistency. Therefore over time a servant leadership model gives way to a top-down leadership model. Cultural preservation requires hierarchical leadership.

Courage
Because of the continual battle to maintain the culture, I see a lessening of courage in the overall spiritual battle the church is waging against the Enemy. It is a large distraction causing strife, divisions and weariness. Ministry lags in courage because of the constant pressure to prevent change of the culture. Needs within the congregation change, without any hope of the church changing to accommodate them. When a cross-cultural seeker enters the picture, it gets more frustrating. This hinders zeal, vitality and courage.

---

[5] Stephen L. Yoder, *My Beloved Brethren* (Self-published, 1992), 8

No Greater Burden

Critical Thinking

Critical thinking in this context does not mean to criticize or to complain. It means to think carefully and continually. It means deep thinking. This is an important ingredient in an active spiritual Kingdom church. We need to be able to think carefully, to insure the church does not drift from the original Kingdom plan. Tradition cannot be relied upon to keep things from "creeping in unawares". In Acts we read:

> *"Then the brethren immediately sent Paul and Silas away by night to Berea. When they arrived, they went in to the synagogue of the Jews. These were more fair minded than those in Thessalonica, in that they received the word with all readiness, and they searched the Scriptures daily to find out whether these things were so."* (Acts 17:11).

They seemed to be willing and ready to be teachable, but with a determination to look at the Scriptures for a careful examination of what they were told. Would we tolerate questioning the teachings and decisions of a leader, let alone an apostle? The Bereans did.

> *"Challenging an apostle was commended, not reproved."*[6]

The Bereans were more inclined to do this than the Thessalonians. So Paul had to remind them of this... "Test all things, hold fast to what is good." (1 Thes. 5:21). He said it even more strongly to the Galatians. "But even if we, or an angel from heaven, preach any other gospel to you than what we have preached to you, let him be accursed." (Gal 1:8). It was important enough to him that he said it twice.

---

[6] Finny Kuruvilla, *King Jesus Claims His Church* (Anchor Cross Publishing 2013), 29

Where Are We?

Youth

Any weaknesses in a church also affect the youth. A culture that overemphasizes marriage and family puts its youth in a category of dormancy. This leaves them waiting to be useful until they are married. This in turn necessitates youth specific activities, restrictions, and focus to keep them in control. The presence of specific guidelines and activities is a symptom of deficiencies in the church vision. Youth need close interaction and purpose. They need something to live and sacrifice for. Many singles find it hard to live and sacrifice for the preservation of the culture alone.

Expectations and Assumptions

The training a child receives, as Solomon observed, forms the foundation of his life. The content and quality of that foundation affects how he thinks, speaks and behaves the rest of his life. It affects his outlook on life and how he interprets the world around him. It affects how he anticipates life when he encounters unknowns. And certainly, if he becomes a seeker, unknowns will be faced. There are unknowns both on the part of the seeker and the part of the plain people he wants to join.

Every culture produces expectations and assumptions. Seekers come with theirs. Plain people have theirs. Seekers can override theirs as long as the balance between perceived gain and loss is on the side of gain. When things change or expectations are not realized, the balance can tip the other way. The result is discouragement that can lead to the exit door. Because of the role that culture plays in human life, seekers will always be a subclass within the plain churches. Seekers will always be seekers.

Following are some assumptions and expectations I observed over the years. This list is not exhaustive and likely not without bias.

Many focus on the relationship between seeker and plain people. You can decide if they are right or wrong, true or false.

Expectations of the Plain People

About Seekers...

- Must conform to, be obedient to, and submit to the church.
- Must give up their talents, background, heritage, culture, understandings of scripture and their individuality.
- They come from the world. (Everything outside the Old Order church is "the world".) Therefore very little they bring with them is useful to us, particularly things relating to Christianity.
- They come to us because all they had and knew is worldly and they want the truth from us.
- Have nothing to offer except service, submission and obedience.
- Are in general not suitable to lead.
- Will always be a seeker. They may someday "look and act just like one of us", but will never "be" us. (Other examples of this thinking are displayed in comments such as "we're glad you are here" or "you do that better than we do."
- Are getting close to being accepted and influential when his children are members, happily married in the church, and their grandchildren are members also.
- Will figure out what to do by observing how we do things.
- If they don't know something, they will ask. It would not be humble for us to tell them how to do something.
- Surely they already know what to do and how to do it.
- If they lose confidence and want to leave, we will not help them relocate because that would weaken our position and message.

Where Are We?

- Should have a willingness to be open about themselves, their journey in life, their faith, their family, etc.
- Should have a desire to participate in as many activities of the church as they can, and get to know the members.
- Should have a desire to live and look like the members do, to the extent possible.
- Should have a humble teachable attitude.
- Should have a respect for our people, faith, practices, walk of life, and our property.

About Other Things
- Training is unwanted. It is unwise and wrong to get teaching and training particularly on spiritual matters and practices. We do not teach or train each other in doctrine or practices. We do not want a trained ministry.
- It is prideful to become knowledgeable about or good at something particularly in spiritual matters.
- Change is not good. The goal is to stay the same. Innovation threatens our culture.
- Our goal is for our culture to be the same for generations.
- Spiritual matters and church practices are the business of the ministry, not the laity.
- We will deal with things when we face them. To anticipate future needs and plan for them is not wise. (Reactive vs. Proactive)
- The goal is to live scripturally, according to our tradition.
- The only two options for conformity are either to the church or to the world.
- Our culture (tradition) prevails over personal understanding of truth.
- A person or group that has similar Anabaptist beliefs, but is outside our fellowship circles is more threatening to us than an unbeliever or those of non-Anabaptist culture.
- Family farming is the best Christian occupation.
- Everyone who joins us has the same goals and vision.

- The picture is bigger than just this one church. We need to follow the decisions and expectations of the fellowship.
- The needs of the church are best met by the decisions of the fellowship.
- Loyalty to the fellowship takes precedence over the needs of the local church.
- The brotherhood will always follow the decisions of the ministry.

Expectations of Seekers
- Be fully accepted (background, heritage, traditions).
- Contribute my ideas, opinions, talents, innovations, etc. for the greater good of the church.
- Help "improve" things.
- Thinks the ministry is always good, right, humble, honest, and trustworthy, absent of politics and wanting to know what my ideas are and use them.
- Want to live a more scriptural life, according to my understanding of Scripture.
- My understanding of Scripture will be accepted.
- Will be recognized for my talents and they will be utilized.
- Will be thanked for my contributions and complimented on my achievements.
- Will be kept informed of what is going on in the church and what is expected of me.
- May someday be considered for ordination.
- The Bible prevails over tradition and culture.
- The goal is to live "the old fashioned" way.
- It is my choice to accept some of the things practiced by the church.
- Most things are optional if I don't agree with them.
- The ministry will always follow the consensus of the brotherhood.
- The church will understand me and the way I think.

Where Are We?

- The church will help solve my struggles, and not cause them.
- The church will function according to how I think it should.
- The church will teach me what I need to know to become fully a part of the church.
- If I have emotional, relational and spiritual difficulties, I will receive loving, relevant and timely help from the church.
- I will make the change from my old culture to the new without much difficulty. I can live this way.
- I want to, can and will give up my traditions, heritage and culture completely.
- Issues of relating to or separation from other Christian groups are up to the individual conscience.
- Someday I will be fully Amish.
- My children will be treated fairly and respectfully in school.
- When my children are old enough to marry, they will be considered equally as potential marriage partners
- Change is good.

Summary

Let me recap before continuing. I shared my observations of how culture has impacted us and other seekers who try to join an Old Order setting. We looked at briefly how a culture can get started, and the effects it has on the Church itself. Depending on your point of view, you may look at these things as positive, intentional traits, or negative, unintentional ones. I hope to avoid making any judgment. I have benefited personally from some of these things. But I'm still nagged by the question of whether or not it is the same vision as Jesus had before He stepped off the earth.

My wife has finished her hot chocolate and has made some progress on her baby outfit. It's hard to realize how much time goes by when I get talking about this. The sun is getting lower in the sky. It's still warm enough to continue with the story. So, if you have patience, I hope to continue with how I think we got here.

Where Are We?

How Did We Get Here?

Part 2 - How Did We Get Here?

I'd like to continue my story by sharing with you some of the things I've discovered while trying to settle my mind. I needed to look at history to get myself oriented. I don't think history is the most reliable source for answering questions, but it does tend to give us the overview we need sometimes. It's not likely to paint a very detailed picture, and is quite subject to interpretations both of the historian and the one reading the history. Sometimes it's only necessary to look at how things were in the beginning and compare them with how they are now. That can reveal a difference. But getting some snapshots of the progress along the way may help understand how we got here. The scope of where Christianity is as a whole is too large to cover in one look. Just an examination of the current state of Anabaptism as a whole is daunting. I believe there are similarities among all Anabaptist groups. But I will focus mostly on the Old Order people, since that is my viewpoint.

No Greater Burden

Early Church

It seems that many conservative churches want to "go back" to the early church to find a firm foundation. There is much about them that we do not know. But there are some writings that give us some indications of their nature, and how they understood the apostle's teachings. Commenting on the closing of the apostolic age and the opening of the ante-Nicene age, historian Philip Schaff says:

> *"The hand of God has drawn a bold line of demarcation between the century of miracles and the succeeding ages, to show, by the abrupt transition and the striking contrast, the difference between the work of God and the work of man, and to impress us the more deeply with the supernatural origin of Christianity and the incomparable value of the New Testament. There is no other transition in history so radical and sudden, and yet so silent and secret."* [1]

After including a quotation from the "Epistle to Diognetus" (see Part III), Schaff writes...

> *"The ante-Nicene age has been ever since the Reformation a battlefield between Catholic and Evangelical historians and polemics, and is claimed by both for their respective creeds. But it is a sectarian abuse of history to identify the Christianity of this martyr period either with Catholicism, or with Protestantism. It is rather the common root out of which both have sprung, Catholicism (Greek and Roman) first, and Protestantism afterwards...the ante-Nicene church is simply the continuation of the apostolic period, and has nothing in common either with the*

---

[1] Philip Schaff, *History of the Christian Church*, Vol 2, (Hendrickson Publishers, 1858), 7

hierarchical, or with the Erastian systems...The church was altogether based on the voluntary principle, as a self-supporting and self-governing body." [2]

Constantine

The marriage of the church with the government was a major turning point in the history of the church. With the creation of this new hybrid of church and state came the virtual removal of the Kingdom concept of Christianity. A new powerful religion was formed. Some of the same Old Testament ways of thinking fit well into this new religion. While the Amish and other Anabaptist groups promote various forms of asceticism, it did not originate from Anabaptism. Early in the Constantine era monastic inclinations grew strong. Again from Philip Schaff:

"Christian life was viewed as consisting mainly in certain outward exercises, rather than an inward disposition, in a multiplicity of acts rather than a life of faith. The great ideal of virtue was, according to the prevailing notion of the fathers and the councils, not so much to transform the world and sanctify the natural things and relations created by God, as to flee from the world into monastic seclusion... All the germs of this asceticism appear in the second half of the third century... Asceticism in general is a rigid outward self-discipline, by which the spirit strives after full dominion over the flesh, and a superior grade of virtue... [3]

---

[2] Philip Schaff, *History of the Christian Church, Vol 2,* (Hendrickson Publishers, 1858),11

[3] Philip Schaff, *History of the Christian Church, Vol 2,* (Hendrickson Publishers, 1858),388

> *It substitutes an abnormal, self-appointed virtue and piety for the normal forms prescribed by the Creator; and not rarely looks down upon the divinely-ordained standard with spiritual pride...It presumes a certain degree of culture, in which man has emancipated himself from the powers of nature and risen to consciousness of his moral calling; but thinks to secure itself against temptation only by entire separation from the world, instead of standing in the world to overcome it and transform it into the Kingdom of God. Asceticism is by no means limited to the Christian church, but it there developed its highest and noblest form. We observe kindred phenomena long before Christ; among the Jews, in the Nazarites, the Essenes, and the cognate Therapeutae, and still more among the heathens, in the old Persian and Indian religions, especially among the Buddhists, who have even a fully developed system of monastic life, which struck some Roman missionaries as the devil's caricature of the Catholic system."* [4]

The things I found interesting here is that the effort to seclude oneself from the "world" is not new. It is an age-old human practice, practiced by many religions, including various forms of Christianity. To claim that a culture based on a form of monastic seclusion represents the "upside down" Kingdom of Christ seems incorrect.

Dark Ages

For over a millennium the Catholic Church maintained an iron grip on the population, armed with the power of the government to

---

[4] Philip Schaff, *History of the Christian Church, Vol 2*, (Hendrickson Publishers, 1858),389

enforce church rules. It was convinced it was the only "right" Christian church. Tradition became the predominant force for the interpretation of right and wrong. The teachings of the theologians and the centuries of enforcing them formed the substance of truth. We see the results of this. It had no power against the indulgence of the flesh. Depravity developed to an ultimate level. Today, we dare not look back and point a finger at the Catholics for this. It is how all men are by their fallen nature. The Bible clearly warns of this, and this part of human history demonstrates it.

Reformation

With the coming of the Reformation this hybrid church/state split into many other forms. I call this the Age of Denominations. The Protestant reformation brought about a restructuring of doctrine, but not necessarily a change of morals. It also did not bring religious freedom. Instead of just the Catholics being married to the state, the Reformed churches were also. But throughout the church age there has always been a faithful remnant of believers clinging to Kingdom principles and maintaining a two kingdom understanding. During the Reformation the Anabaptists held that distinction. They started well, but the difficult climate of that era took its toll on them.

> *"Intense persecution distanced the Anabaptists from the interpretive principles they had shared with the Protestants... And without their early leaders who worked through these principles, in an ironic twist, the Anabaptists would partly return to Roman Catholic views. In addition, they grew suspicious of learning and favored survival instead of advance. The grand dreams of Grebel and his co-*

workers for total church renewal shrank to a defensive congregationalism."[5]

This view is echoed by Peter Hoover. Again, after starting out well, changes came that set the movement backwards:

> *After Menno Simons excommunicated Lambert Kramer, Zelis Jacobs, and all the Swiss and south German brothers with them in 1559, the Anabaptist movement entered a time of confusion and distress. What Zwingli, Luther, and the Pope could not accomplish through force, the terrible abuse of brotherhood authority accomplished in the space of a few years.*
>
> *In the north, the movement broke into dozens of quarrelling fragments. In the south, many got discouraged and fell away. Thousands of Anabaptists, including most of those in the lower Rhein area, gave up and joined the state churches.* <u>*Among those who remained (mainly in out-of-the-way rural areas in France and Switzerland), Jakob Amman introduced the same disastrous teaching.*</u> *Then the proud spirit of "we are the ones who own the truth" and "following Christ means submitting to us" was carried by what was left of the Mennonites, the Amish and the Hutterites to America to reproduce itself a hundredfold there.*[6]

This helped me see that even before coming to America; the seeds were sown for a change of thinking. The American religious soil would help these thoughts sprout and grow well. I see a similarity between their "suspicion of learning" and our dislike for education beyond the 8th grade. I also see the shift from "advance" (which I understand to be the proclamation of the Gospel) to survival,

---

[5] Finny Kuruvilla, **King Jesus Claims His Church**, Anchor Cross Publishing, 69

[6] Peter Hoover, *The Secret of the Strength.* Primitive Christianity Publishers, 2008.

which promoted the development of a safe and comfortable ethnic environment. The move to America (where English was the national language) made it easier for them to use their German language to enhance that form of separation.

For the Amish, a turning point seems to have occurred with the falling out between Jacob Amman and Hans Reist. In responding to the disagreement between himself and Reist, Amman took a firm position, attempting to teach an uncompromising gospel. Anthropologist John Hostetler observed that Amman;

> *"...had no patience with the deliberations of those who would not make up their minds immediately. Aware of the dangers of compromise faced by the Alsatian congregations, Amman demanded that all return to a stricter discipline. One result of this position was the creation of a cohesive group with a particular ethnic composition...Amman's emphasis on orthodoxy and on more frequent practice of the rituals led to stronger cohesion but also to greater legalism. Amman was able to win the Alsatian congregations to his views most likely because they sensed that their ranks needed to be firmly tightened if they were going to retain their distinctive identity."*[7]

I could see in this as a spirit of contention which caused the creation of "a cohesive group with a particular ethnic composition". Also notice the intent to "retain their distinctive identity". How unlike the Christian command to be "in the world, but not of it"! Hostetler further expands on this defining event...

> *"The Amish cleavage was not unlike the formation of other social movements. Certain characteristics are common*

---

[7] John A. Hostetler, **Amish Society**, The Johns Hopkins University Press, 1993, 40-41

to all leaders, prophets or founders who establish dissenting movements. Sectarian movements tend to emerge from the following conditions:

- *A sectarian movement must establish an ideology difference from that of the parent group. Amman succeeded in making Meidung a major issue that precipitated a cleavage.*

- *A sense of urgency is vocalized by an authoritarian person who imposes negative sanction on opposing persons or groups. Amman could not follow a middle course and he would not respond to those who fell on their knees to beg for patience.*

- *The goals of a sect must be specific rather than general if they are to gain acceptance. Broadly defined goals give room for personal interpretation, but specific goals demand uncompromising conformity. Amman's specific and attainable goals defined a new order.*

- *A sect must establish cultural separatism by invoking symbolic, material, and ideological differences from those of the parental group. The symbols of separation in Amman's group took the form of different styles of dress, grooming, and physical appearance. For Amman, doctrinal matters had to take on visible and explicit, not just "spiritual" character. Nonconformity to the world meant not only a difference in thought and in the heart but also an outward material separation as characterized by Amman's emphasis on the avoidance of "worldly" hair, beard, and dress styles.*

In the course of their natural history, the Amish have proved similar to other social movements in four ways:

How Did We Get Here?

1) *They attempted to change or keep from changing certain beliefs or practices among existing groups;*

2) *They appealed to the people as a means of achieving their goals and thereby distributed responsibility among followers and leaders according to the vision or skill of the dominant leader, which resulted in;*

3) *They had a geographical scope that transcended the local community and;*

4) *They had a persistence through time.*

The Amish achieved all these features. The persistence of custom, its slow response to change, is a distinctive feature of the Amish people. Through it we can observe how Amish society has remained relatively stable while the dominant society has changed radically." [8]

I couldn't help noticing several important things here. Amman's group

- Was a social movement.

- Had religious motivations.

- Was a new *religious order*.
    "A **religious order** is a lineage of communities and organizations of people who live in some way set apart from society in accordance with their specific religious devotion, usually characterized

---

[8] John A. Hostetler, *Amish Society*, The Johns Hopkins University Press, 1993, 48-49

by the principles of its founder's religious practice."
Wikipedia

- Demanded uncompromising conformity.

- Required symbols of separation from the parent group in terms of physical appearance.

- Was a sect.
  A sect is a group that deviates from the "right" religion. In reality, the "right" religion could be the wrong one, or it could be the dominant one. The Gnostics could be thought of as a sect deviating from the right "right" religion, whereas the early Anabaptists were a sect deviating from the wrong "right" religion. I'm not trying to imply here that Reist was the right or wrong group, just that Amman's effort to make his point, if he did not begin it, strengthened the Old Order Amish view of cultural separation.

One of Amman's contemporaries had a similar observation. In the area of clothing, as an example of this trend, Gerrit Roosen wrote in 1697:

> *I am truly sorry that you have been disturbed by people who exalt themselves and make rules about things not clearly laid down in the Gospel. If the apostles had told us exactly how and with what the believer is to clothe himself, then we would have a case to work on. But we dare not contradict the Gospel by forcing men's consciences about certain styles of hats, clothes, shoes, stockings or haircuts. Things are done differently in every country. We dare not excommunicate people just because they do not line up to our customs. We dare not put them out of the church as sinful leaven, when neither Jesus nor the apostles bound us in matters of outward form. Neither Jesus nor the apostles*

made rules or laws about such things. Rather, Paul said in Col. 2 that we do not inherit the kingdom of heaven through food and drink. Neither do we inherit it through the form and cut of our clothes.

Jesus did not bind us in outward things. Why does our friend Jakob Amman undertake to make rules, then exclude those from the church who do not keep them? If he considers himself a servant of the Gospel but wants to live by the letter of outward law, then he should not have two coats. He should not carry money in his pocket nor shoes on his feet. If he does not live according to the letter of Jesus' law, how can he force the brothers to live by the letter of his own laws? Oh that he would follow Paul who feared God, who treated people gently and who took pains not to offend the conscience of the weak... Paul did not write one word about outward forms of clothing. But he taught us to be conformed to those of low estate and imitate only that which is honorable. We are to do that within the manner of the land in which we live. We are to shun styles and proud worldliness (1 John 2). We should not be quick to change our manner of dress. Fashion deserves rebuke. New articles of dress should not be accepted until they become common practice in the land, and then only if they are becoming to Christian humility.

I do not walk in the lust of the eyes and worldliness. All my life I have stuck to one style of dress. But suppose I should have dressed myself according to another custom, the way they do it in another land? Should I then be excommunicated? That would be illogical and against the Scriptures.

The Scriptures must be our guide. We dare not run ahead of them. We must follow them, not lightheartedly, but in carefulness and fear. It is dangerous to step into the place of God's judgment and bind on earth what is not bound in heaven.⁹

American Religious Environment

The religious freedom America offered the Anabaptists gave them hope of life without persecution. But in reality, it expanded the forms of persecution from merely physical to spiritual and emotional persecution. These came in forms not as easily recognized, including prosperity, freedom of conscience and choices, freedom to be isolated and safe, temptation to individualism, and a host of choices of different religious persuasions. Many of these persuasions were not clearly distinguishable from their own. The American experiment had great influence on the Anabaptists.

> *"Having been preoccupied with their farms, the Mennonites' focus became narrow. They remained an unlearned people and could not effectively compete with the charismatic evangelists that roamed the countryside. They were content with their prosperous farms and some form of their traditional faith. However, their spiritual candle was burning too low."* [10]

> *"Mennonites interpreted discipleship more and more in terms of adhering to their own group's discipline and practices, and less and less in the language of spreading the rule of the Lord in the world."* [11]

---

[9] Hoover, Chapter 20 (Quoting from *Abschrift von Gerhard Rosen von Hamburg. Den 21. Dezember, 1697*)

[10] ***Joy In Submission,*** Donald Martin, Vineyard Publications, 73

[11] Martin, 73 (Quoting from **Land, Piety, Peoplehood,** Richard K. MacMaster, 1985, 167)

How Did We Get Here?

> "American individualism clashes with the Anabaptist theme of Gelassenheit or yieldedness to God and the church. Without a good understanding of Gelassenheit, voluntary church order is impossible. Therefore when the Mennonites embraced individualism, church order lost its voluntary principles and became rule-based. Guidelines only work as long as people are willing to voluntarily submit to the group's standards."[12]

Notice the connection between individualism and rule-based thinking. This goes deeper and affects us more than appears on the surface. This is an irony that seems to be opposite of what it should. We have equated Gelassenheit with a rule-based approach, not a voluntary approach. It's interesting to notice the difference the author makes between rule-based and voluntary principles. He equates these with guidelines. Voluntary principles / guidelines are bible based. Rule-based thinking is based on the commandments of men.

> "With time Fundamentalism influenced the church leaders so that they were inclined to legislate the church's guidelines until they became laws. The concept that Christian living is a voluntary service for Christ was weakened by the authoritarian approach of Mennonite Fundamentalism...This issue of 'legislated Christian living' versus voluntary discipleship, continues to muddy the waters for the Conservatives and the Old Order Mennonites."[13]

Here, legislated Christian living opposes voluntary brotherhood. Not only in the nature of how it is administered, but the basis of the administration. One uses commandments of men, which create visible and measurable cultural distinctions, and the other uses

---

[12] Martin, 120

[13] Martin, 106

biblical principles which do not produce culture and are hard to measure, but produces holiness within *any* culture.

> *"The Mennonite Fundamentalists transformed nonconformity from the former voluntary principle of submission, into a biblical teaching that was being legislated more and more over the years.'Aggresso-conservatives (Mennonite Fundamentalists) understood nonconformity, particularly in dress, to protect them from insidious worldliness even as they moved purposefully into more involvement with the surrounding culture.' They believed that their distinctive clothes and regulations would help them retain separation as they moved into general society."* [14]

> *"Preaching styles changed dramatically from the early American era of persecution and humility theology where Bible verses were loosely linked to highlight general themes and delivered with humble admonitions.*
>
> *Fundamentalist literalism now allowed preachers to clearly explicate specific scriptures that would 'support and encourage' uniformity of belief and practice and were delivered with rational proofs and a rhetoric that demanded a response.*

---

[14] Andrew C. Martin, Thesis, *Creating A Timeless Tradition, The Effects of Fundamentalism on the Conservative Mennonite Movement*, (Waterloo, Canada, 2007), 134

How Did We Get Here?

> *The inherited practice of church discipline also came to play an increasing role as a way of implementing uniform nonconformity."*[15]

I couldn't help noticing that Fundamentalism played a part in this change of thought. Mennonite Fundamentalism included the necessity of creating a cultural divide between "the world" and themselves. We seem to have adopted this same way of thinking probably because of our desire to move away from general society.

It is also useful to note that like other groups, the use of church discipline to produce uniform nonconformity developed and became a powerful tool for maintaining the Fundamentalist culture. Social sanctions are a very useful means of controlling groups of people. They are a natural means, however, not a spiritual one.

---

[15] Andrew C. Martin, Thesis, *Creating A Timeless Tradition, The Effects of Fundamentalism on the Conservative Mennonite Movement*, (Waterloo, Canada, 2007), 68

No Greater Burden

Summary

I realize I'm trying to come to a conclusion based on fragmented knowledge. With all the dynamics of interpersonal relationship, biblical interpretations, interaction and perceived threats of other church groups, it's difficult to clearly define why churches reach the positions they do. Despite that, I see some distinct shapes in the fog...

- The perceived threat of becoming worldly has motivated the conservative Anabaptists to retreat. The motivation to spread the Gospel news is lessened. This began before the move to America.

- The natural human inclination to establish uniformity within groups strongly affects the Anabaptists, particularly the Old Order groups. Jacob Amman seems to have strengthened this approach.

- Anabaptist history in America seems to be a study of continuous reaction. It seems to demonstrate what happens when using the previous generation, (or the surrounding religious climate) as a pattern for what to be like or not like. Each new group forms out of reaction to others, and continually becomes more distorted from the original pattern. Many look to Anabaptist history and try to find answers to today's challenges based on how some group in the past handled a similar problem. This results in continual distortion and an illusion of correctness. Modern Anabaptism tends to forget to look beyond their own history for answers.

I would like to say at this point that I am grateful to be living in such a beautiful setting with such good neighbors. I value their presence even if I don't express it. I continue to ponder my cultural

How Did We Get Here?

dilemma. In the midst of blessings something stirs me to question where the privilege of having a safe, comfortable and perpetual ethnic society comes from. Did God grant it? Does God require it? Is God pleased with it? Can I in good conscience continue this way?

The sun is getting low on the horizon. Our horse is heading to the barn in expectation of her evening meal. My wife has gone inside because it is getting chilly out. In the meantime, I need to go do chores and feed the horse. But if you are still willing, when I come back, I hope to share with you some possible options. See you then.

Where Do We Go From Here?

Part 3 - Where Do We Go From Here?

The chores are done. As I was walking up from the barn, I couldn't help noticing the beautiful Maine sunset we have this evening. The reds and pinks seem to make the fall colors even more vivid. I'd really appreciate a cup of hot chocolate now, but I know it would just get cold while I finish my story. Let me continue.

A Starting Point

The Bible

To know where to go, we need guidance. Consider how Christians in America have many cultures, many with ethnic distinctions. Christianity beautifies any culture. It is not one of its own. The evils of the world are a result of people being people. The Roman culture in Jesus time was not much better, if any, than modern American culture. It is a result of the corrupt heart of man. Paul gives us guidance by making it clear that he did not intend for Christians to "go out of the world" to avoid its evil culture...

> *"I wrote to you in my epistle not to keep company with sexually immoral people. Yet I certainly did not mean with*

> *the sexually immoral people of this world, or with the covetous, or extortioners, or idolaters, since then you would need to go out of the world." (1 Cor. 5:10).*

The idea here seems to be that we can't and shouldn't try to escape the world physically. Remember the concept of being in the world but not of it? The idea is of being in or out. Monastic societies try to be "out" of the world, physically isolating themselves from the world to establish moral purity. But impurity is inside of men, and Paul seems to be saying here that it can't be escaped this way. The "upside down" aspect of the Kingdom is that it cleanses men's hearts from the world within them, not by keeping them from being inside the world. Being "of the world" is to have the world inside of them. Paul emphasizes this unique aspect of the Gospel in the same passage of Corinthians...

> *"But now I have written to you not to keep company with anyone named a brother, who is a fornicator, or covetous, or an idolater, or a reviler, or a drunkard, or an extortioner...not even to eat with such a person." (1 Cor. 5:11)*

Isn't this interesting? He's not saying to isolate oneself from the greater society, but the opposite. He seems to be telling us to isolate ourselves from *other Christians* who are not in fellowship with Christ. Or, more specifically, to isolate the errant brother. The point seems apparent...if the world is in a believer's heart, it needs to be dealt with there, in the heart. In this case the context is the body of Christ and the evil is to be ejected from it to keep it pure. This needs to be done redemptively, with the intended purpose to assist in cleansing the heart of the errant brother. But it doesn't work for the body (the church) to isolate itself from the world around it. The same is true for individuals. Evil needs to be purged from the heart to make it pure. This is only accomplished by the inward washing of the Word and the blood of Christ. That washing cannot be accomplished simply by isolating oneself from the world around him.

The apostle Peter also gives another view of this from a different angle. He speaks of God offering us a divine nature, along with all the tools necessary for life and godliness. He tells us where the wickedness of the world comes from; it is our own hearts! The King James Version uses the word lust, which means a strong desire. In this case it refers to evil desires...

> *"According as his divine power hath given unto us all things that pertain unto life and godliness, through the knowledge of him that hath called us to glory and virtue: Whereby are given unto us exceeding great and precious promises: that by these ye might be partakers of the divine nature, having escaped the corruption that is in the world through lust." (2 Pet 1:4-5)*

"Through lust." The world is corrupted through lust. The world does not cause lust. Things around us do not cause lust. Evil desires well from the heart, as Jesus said in Mark 7. It is not what goes into a man that defiles him, but rather what comes out of him, from within his heart. Evil originates within. What we learn from this is that efforts of the flesh to escape the corruption that is in the world do not work. They can't. Peter says we are able to escape the corruption by the exceedingly great and precious promises, incorporated in the divine power given to us through Christ. Paul David Tripp puts it this way...

> *"A subtle monasticism still exists in the church today. The theology of the monastery taught, 'It's an evil world out there, so the way to be pure is to separate from it.' Yet history records that the monastery duplicated all the ills of the surrounding society. Why? Because they made a tragic mistake: They let people in! And as sinful people came in,*

they brought with them the full range of evil desires, corrupting the very environment that was their hope of purity."[1]

The means of escaping this corruption is not through isolation from the outworking of corruption, but through the divine power Peter tells us about, the power that changes the corrupt heart. This divine power allows us to be partakers of the divine nature, which enables godliness and virtue. Godliness and virtue are active products of a heart that worships God.

An Example from Early Christianity

I have a 10 volume set of writings from early Christians. In Volume 1 I find a short writing sandwiched between "*The First Epistle of Clement*" and "*The Epistle of Polycarp to the Philippians*" called "*The Epistle to Diognetus*". This anonymous letter is considered by historians to be a "gem of purest ray" as it relates to the authenticity and trustworthiness of the author. It ranks with Clement and Polycarp. In this writing, estimated to have been written in AD 130, the author takes time to make a remarkable assessment of the Christian walk of life in the 2nd century. It is most revealing, and sums up New Testament teachings well. Let's break it up into two parts. The first describes what Christians are not:

> "*For the Christians are distinguished from other men neither by country, nor language, nor the customs which they observe. For they neither inhabit cities of their own, nor employ a peculiar form of speech, nor lead a life which is marked out by any singularity. The course of conduct which they follow has not been devised by any speculation or deliberation of inquisitive men; nor do they, like some, proclaim themselves the advocates of any merely human*

---

[1] Paul David Tripp, ***Instruments In The Redeemer's Hands***, P&R Publishing, 2002, 265

doctrines. But inhabiting Greek as well as barbarian cities, according as the lot of each of them has determined, and following the customs of the natives in respect to clothing, food, and the rest of their ordinary conduct, they display to us their wonderful and confessedly striking method of life." [2]

What can we learn from this?
- They don't have their own country, nor their own city.
- They don't have a distinct language or form of speech.
- They don't have distinct customs.
- They don't have practices marked by any peculiarity.
- Their conduct has not been devised by any man-made distinctives.
- They don't proclaim any human doctrines.
- They inhabit cities, Greek and barbarian.
- They follow the customs of natives in regard to food, clothing, and ordinary conduct.
- In general these all pertain to the outward visible effects of culture, which they did not define. Key phrases used here are: "marked out by any singularity"; "speculation or deliberation of inquisitive men"; "merely human doctrines." These in my mind, point to wonderful and noble efforts by people to create godly societies. But as noted by the author, these were not seen as the marks of Christian conduct.

What does this tell us about non-conformity? Are we able to grasp the impact of this? They had a different view of separation than we do. Isn't the author telling us that they had no self-determined culture? From many angles they look like all the rest of society. They did not seem to view a distinct cultural identity as a means of achieving non-conformity. They were not *physically* separated from those in the world. This physical identity is created by the use of

---

[2] *Epistle To Diognetus*, Ante-Nicene Fathers, Vol 1, (Hendrickson Publishers), 69

defined and enforced applications of principles to create a visible uniformity. It might be natural to wonder how Christians, without a distinctive *physical* identity, can be salt and light in the world. The second part reveals how separation is accomplished...

> *"They dwell in their own countries, but simply as sojourners. As citizens, they share in all things with others, and yet endure all things as if foreigners. Every foreign land is to them as their native country, and every land of their birth as a land of strangers. They marry, as do all [others]; they begat children; but they do not destroy their offspring. They have a common table, but not a common bed. They are in the flesh, but they do not live after the flesh. They pass their days on earth, but they are citizens of heaven. They obey the prescribed laws, and at the same time surpass the laws by their lives. They love all men, and are persecuted by all. They are unknown and condemned; they are put to death, and restored to life. They are poor, yet make many rich; they are in lack of all things, and yet abound in all; they are dishonored, and yet in their very dishonor are glorified. They are evil spoken of, and yet are justified; they are reviled, and bless; they are insulted, and repay the insult with honor; they do good, yet are punished as evil-doers. When punished, they rejoice as if quickened into life; they are assailed by the Jews as foreigners, and are persecuted by the Greeks; yet those who hate them are unable to assign any reason for their hatred.*
>
> *To sum up all in one word -- what the soul is in the body, that are the Christians in the world. The soul is dispersed through all the members of the body, and Christians are scattered through all the cities of the world. The soul dwells in the body, yet is not of the body; and Christians dwell in the world, yet are not of the world. The invisible soul is guarded by the visible body, and Christians are known indeed to be in the world, but their godliness*

remains invisible. The flesh hates the soul, and wars against it, though itself suffering no injury, because it is prevented from enjoying pleasures; the world also hates the Christians, though in nowise injured, because they abjure pleasures. The soul loves the flesh that hates it, and [loves also] the members; Christians likewise love those that hate them. The soul is imprisoned in the body, yet preserves that very body; and Christians are confined in the world as in a prison, and yet they are the preservers of the world."[3]

What are the distinguishing marks noted by the author? Are they not attitudes, motives, and issues of the heart? This results in the things observed by the author. They defined a way of responding to the environment around them that is holy and acceptable to God. It was a way of thinking. This is the nonconformity God requires. Isn't this the essence of the "upside down" kingdom? I believe that any group that defines cultural behavior is behaving naturally, according to human thinking. It is difficult to avoid. We all want things spelled out. But didn't Jesus design a different way? He made it possible to be distinct (not of the world) within the mass of humanity (in the world) in ways the author says is "confessedly striking". Isn't this what "in the world" means? This is not describing an easy, safe or comfortable lifestyle. It is dangerous.

In history, this has resulted in persecution. It is a paradox to think that people can stand out in a crowd without looking any different. This is opposite natural thinking. Christianity has standards that cannot be followed by the flesh alone. They are spiritually accomplished, as the above observation beautifully displays for us. Visible cultural standards (applications) can be faked. But genuine Biblical standards (principles) have no loopholes and cannot be faked. They are unnatural. This is what the second part of this writing tells me. It is significant. Separation is not simply the

---

[3] *Epistle To Diognetus*, Ante-Nicene Fathers, Vol 1, (Hendrickson Publishers), 70

obedience to extra biblical standards outwardly, but obedience to biblical standards inwardly, resulting in a walk of life which demonstrate the principles outwardly. The walk demonstrates the talk, which comes from the heart. But I keep coming back to the question...who defines the walk? The "*Epistle To Diognetus*" seems to shout the answer. This is the difference between the first and second quoted sections.

Isn't it the same today? Is the church today supposed to operate differently than it did then? The responsibility of each child of God is to be willingly obedient. How can we do this if it is mandated upon pain of excommunication and other social sanctions, rather than by free will?

Here are some other views on this epistle:

> *"The community of Christians thus from the first felt itself, in distinction from Judaism and from heathenism, the salt of the earth, the light of the world, the city of God set on a hill, the immortal soul in a dying body; and this its impression respecting itself was no proud conceit, but truth and reality, acting in life and in death, and opening the way through hatred and persecution even to an outward victory over the world."* [4]

> *It must be said here, and with considerable emphasis, that the New Testament vision of societal composition did not lead to any attitude of aloofness from the workaday things. We point this out here because the notion is abroad that they who take the New Testament seriously at this point must of necessity become nonchalant concerning the affairs of public life. The aloofness which is characteristic of*

---

[4] **History of the Christian Church, Vol 2**, Philip Schaff, Hendrickson Publishers, 1858, 10

the medieval and modern "sects", an aloofness about which men have often complained, and not without cause, was not a feature of the early Christians. Aloof Christianity comes later and then by way of reaction. No, early Christianity was not aloof; it was deeply involved in the affairs of society. The testimony of The Epistle to Diognetus is enough, it seems, to bear this out. This literary product, which according to modern scholarship dates from near the end of the second century, draws a parallel between the soul and the body on the one hand and the Christians and society on the other hand. Early Christianity, it may be said, took seriously Jesus' idea about "in the world but not of the world." It knew that it was the Master's will that they be "the salt of the earth", a formula that speaks of deep differences going hand in hand with close integration." [5]

Leonard Verduin, also referencing the same *"Epistle To Diognetus,"* reminds us in a slightly different way that Christians were interactive and involved with those around them. The setting was ancient Rome, a pagan, corrupt, sensual, idolatrous, and materialistic society, similar to modern America. Aloofness (a disregard for and a disinterest in things around them) was not a feature of Christianity in ancient Rome. A safe, separated society did not enter their thinking.

An Example from the Reformation
We can see an example of how early Anabaptists viewed this in Article XIX of the **"Confession of Faith According to the Holy Word of God"**, written around 1600 AD. See Appendix 1 for the complete text. I would like to focus on a few key statements…

---

[5] Leonard Verduin, **Reformers and Their Stepchildren**, Christian Hymnary Publishers, 26

> *"Of the signs of the church of God, by which it may be distinguished from all other peoples, we confess the following: In the first place, all true Christians are known by the only saving faith, which works by love. It is wrought, through the grace of God, in the heart of man by the hearing of the Word of God, and hence, is not founded and built upon human decrees, but upon the Word of God alone."*

> *"The church, or the believers, are known by the good works which they evince as fruits of gratitude from their faith; which may not be done according to human instructions, in a self-selected holiness, but in which we follow Christ and His apostles, as they prescribed and walked."*

> *"And as all soldiers forsake their former avocation, and wear the livery of their Lord and king, as a sign to distinguish them from all strange servants, and that they are bound to their captain even unto death, so also, must all true servants of Jesus Christ be armed with the aforesaid marks, that thereby they may be known and distinguished from all other people. But, where said marks do not exist, and where the ordinances of men are the rule of action, there is no church of God, but a vain boasting of the same."*[6]

Notice here the opening statement. It states: "…**by which it may be distinguished from all other peoples:**" The purpose of this article defines clearly what it is that distinguishes Christians from the rest of humanity. This is significant to this discussion because it addresses a key question in my mind. Namely, what did the early Anabaptists understand the Bible's position to be on how they should differ from society around them? It apparently was an issue to them, just like it is to us today.

---

[6] Thieleman J. van Bracht, **Martyrs Mirror**, Herald Press, 1660, 393

Where Do We Go From Here?

In summarizing the article, the authors felt so strongly about this that they made a clear statement. Those churches which used ordinances of men as the defining mark, and not the ones stated in the article were not the church of God. Remember what the "aforesaid marks" were: saving faith, second birth, good works, virtues, and obedience to Christ, faithful ministers, unfeigned godly love, charity, and non-resistance.

Refocusing

Here are a few thoughts on where we should try to be...

> *"Authentic Christianity is firmly committed to the idea of nonsameness, to the idea that people are never to be thought of as all being in the same category in the matter of ultimate convictions. Authentic Christianity sees human society as composite, that is, consisting of people of diverse ways of thinking. It does not expect to encounter unanimity in human society; it expects to find some men stumbling at the very same cross in which other men glory. Totalitarian systems, on the other hand, view all members of a given society as basically unanimous; such systems can thus arise only in a climate in which authentic Christianity has either lapsed or has never been. If this is correct, authentic Christianity is the only viable alternative to totalitarianism."* [7]

The idea of "human societies" the author is speaking of here refers to groups of people. Christianity is about groups of people, members of Christ's kingdom. His view is that all people are different, but human thinking tends to want everyone to be the same.

---

[7] Leonard Verduin, ***Anatomy of a Hybrid***, The Christian Hymnary Publishers,

> "...they (Mennonites) tried openly to make them communities of harmony which rested not on force but on members voluntarily grasping and living by the moral structure of God's creation."[8]

In this situation, members of the Church voluntarily conform to God's moral code. This is to be distinguished from a social code, which ultimately defines a culture. Similarly, our standards of applications forms a social code, and are predominately cultural.

Three Options

It's one thing to realize where one is, but it's another to know what to do about it. To help give some direction, let's zoom out a bit to include the Plain People as a whole. Considering all of this, it seems helpful to share something that Donald Martin expressed in "Joy in Submission"...

> "The Plain People have three options. Will they build their brotherhood on a voluntary yieldedness to live by the moral structure of God's church? Or will they shore up the Mennonite traditions by using Fundamentalism's legalistic and militant approach? Or will they abandon the Scriptural principle of separation from the world and follow evangelical Christianity." [9]

This says it well for me. Even though we are not Mennonites, the thoughts apply. This is how I understand him...

➢ Option 1

---

[8] Donald Martin (Quoting from *Peace, Faith, Nation*, Theron F. Schlabach, 1988, 209)

[9] Donald Martin, *Joy In Submission*, Vineyard Publications, 117

Where Do We Go From Here?

- Return to the original multi-cultural brotherhood. Live by yieldedness to a brotherhood based on biblical standards (principles).

➤ Option 2

- Continue to with live with hierarchical leadership based on Fundamentalist standards (applications).

➤ Option 3

- Follow the pattern of worldly churches with no standards (individualism).

Notice these three options revolve around standards: In the first option, there are biblical standards. These are the ones we can read in the bible. The New Testament has over 900 of them. They tell us how to live the Christian life by giving us principles. They address any situation that may arise in our lives, and tell us how to please God. They do not define specifics. These principles fit in any earthly culture. Where an earthly culture displeases God, the principles address that. There are no loopholes.

With the second option, there are cultural standards. These are derived by people, usually with the best of intentions. For Old Order churches, they are meant to describe how to put into "shoe leather" the principles of the bible. But while we may have good intentions, the wisdom of men never achieves the intended goal. Jesus, I believe, never intended for these to be defined en-mass for the church. They are a matter of liberty. If not allowed to be a matter of liberty, they create cultures. Paul seemed to make it clear that this does not achieve our goal of holy living and denial of the flesh…

No Greater Burden

> *"Therefore, if you died with Christ from the basic principles of the world, why, as though living in the world, do you subject yourselves to regulations...'Do not touch, do not taste, do not handle', which all concern things which perish with the using...according to the commandments and doctrines of men? These things indeed have an appearance of wisdom in self-imposed religion, false humility, and neglect of the body, but are of no value against the indulgence of the flesh."* (Col 2:20-23).

I shared earlier what history says about ascetic and monastic philosophies. They are not necessarily spiritual concepts. They are basic principles of the world; human attempts to achieve spiritual goals. In this passage, Paul clearly defines what this means, consistent with his emphasis on living according to the things of the Spirit (these are the biblical principles we follow). The context of this is in relation to Jewish laws, and the effects they had on the Colossian believers. They seemed confused as to the place the law played in their lives. They were in danger of being deceived.

If we live according to the flesh, we will set our minds on the things of the flesh. So if we have died to the flesh, why do we still subject ourselves to regulations (ordinances defined by people) that focus on and are based on the things of the flesh? They will not help us much because they are after the flesh (they also focus on the flesh), since, as he says, these regulations concern the things which perish with the using, thus they are not spiritual. (Things which are spiritual do not perish with the using.) They are according to the commandments and doctrines of men. And even when they are intended for noble purposes, such as containing the lusts of the flesh, they still do not achieve the intended results and indeed they cannot. This is because indulgences of the flesh originate from the heart, with idolatry at the root. The heart must change in order for behavior to change. No change in behavior means no change in the heart. A change in behavior can be forced by the use of regulations, but does not necessarily reflect a change in heart. That simply addresses symptoms. The flesh can be forced to give the appearance of righteousness, but in truth, as Paul says, it gives "an appearance of wisdom in self-imposed religion, false humility and neglect of the body", which is asceticism. It is a fleshly effort, and therefore of no value against the indulgence of the flesh.

The desire to create a group identity is also a strong motivator to establish rules of uniform practice. This has a strong influence on people. It does tend to create a sense of belonging. This tendency is also a normal human desire. Much has been written about it. People have created many ways to accomplish this throughout history. It's important, however, to recognize that while not necessarily a bad thing, nor prohibited in scripture, it tends to develop into something unintended, and have the unintended results as we have already discussed. People tend to have a natural desire to belong to a group. I think this is why some are drawn to Old Order groups. They have created a society based on some good things. But it seems to me that there is a strong temptation among some Christians to turn this into a requirement for salvation, and a measure of one's relationship to God. That's where the danger lies. It has a way of producing an illusion of things (spiritual life and holiness) that may not actually be present. In a sense, the culture takes precedence over people.

Self-denial is a Christian virtue, but it represents purity only if motivated by a pure heart. Forced denial does not necessarily mean purity. Therefore, mandatory standards based on applications of principles, in the long run achieves only the formation of cultures. They look good, and provide some temporal advantages, but are little value against the indulgences of the flesh (Col 2:23).

The third option is usually the first option people think of when considering the alternative to standards of applications. This is the "no standards" route. This is not an option for Christians. But in order to be clear, I do not intend to imply that having no standards of applications means having no standards. Standards still need to be defined, but they need to be ones that Jesus defined, not ones that people defined to augment the ones Jesus gave. And just because they are in the bible, and we say we follow them, doesn't necessarily mean we are unified in our understanding of them. They need to be discussed and written down if necessary. Clement of Alexandria did something similar to this in his writing called "The Instructor" (Ante-Nicene Fathers, Vol 2). He illustrated many principles with examples. A church needs to be clear on its understandings of principles. This takes communication and work to establish. This is of primary importance.

Renewal

Considering the deep roots that have grown over generations, I believe it would take serious, painful determination for a church to examine itself and chart a new course. How could people undo unquestioned cultural practices that are safe and comfortable? Why would they want to? Their societal structure depends on that time-proven culture. Believing a culture needs to be defined and preserved for many generations is a hard thing to overcome. The belief that standards of applications are the same as biblical standards causes us to believe that having no standards of applications is the same as having no faith or salvation. It would be difficult for an existing church to have the courage and united vision to rethink this. It would take a strong resolve to go back to the original kingdom plan that Jesus intended for His church. It would not do to simply look back over a few hundred years of history and correct a few mistakes. History will not reveal them like a fresh look at the original plan would. For an existing church to do this would require universal motivation. It would require a complete re-evaluation. The leadership would need to examine its own leadership practices, motivations and methods. It would need to open itself to the brotherhood for selfless examination. The brotherhood would need to do the same. Evaluating foundational premises would be difficult and painful. There would likely be casualties.

The magnitude of this is huge. It's a dilemma very much like the situation in the days of the Reformation. It involves loyalties. On the one hand was loyalty to the New Testament scriptures, which knew no Church other than the believer's Church, a church based on personal faith. On the other hand was loyalty to the Catholic Church which developed over time and history, with a great deal of tradition and heritage. Only by ignoring history -- twelve centuries of it -- could the dilemma be escaped...unless one was prepared to repudiate the New Testament. The latter option the Reformers were unwilling to take. The Roman Church had developed the attitude they were correct, being able to cite 12 centuries of history and tradition behind it. It was unwilling to examine itself because there would be too much to lose. To some it was obvious the Church had taken a wrong turn 1200 years earlier and built on sand. Likewise, with us there is a loyalty to three centuries of heritage and tradition. Today there is a similar situation involving conflicting loyalties to heritage and the New Testament. Should we be like the Catholics of the Reformation period, and see no conflict between those two, or recognize the conflict and do something about it? How do you look at it?

A Redeemable Situation
If we see the conflict, regardless of whether we are an existing church[10] or a newly forming one, we can go forward. If there is a

---

[10] I need to mention here that I don't think it's impossible for an existing church to make the necessary changes. It is just harder. Some Old Order groups, particularly newly formed ones, have some impressive visions. They have noble goals. A key change in their approach would involve disconnecting their standards of applications from sanctions. In other words, life style issues would need to be optional, and not mandatory. This would involve not making standardized dress styles, architectural styles, uses of various forms of mechanization and technology tests of membership. Depending on the spiritual strength of the group, this would not necessarily need to result in immediate visible changes, but may likely over time. The bulk of work would then shift from maintenance of the culture, to the building up of the lives of the people in the church. I think such an approach could result in a group retaining an Old Order flavor, as long as the people in the group individually wished to do so.

willingness to return to the original plan and live by yieldedness to a brotherhood based on biblical standards, the situation is redeemable.

Starting New As A Group

Here are a few ideas are about how to begin. Most of them will require spending considerable time together as a group, working it through. If you are not used to this, it may take time getting used to interacting with one another. Like anything else, it would take practice. I hope you will bear with me in this. I'm not an expert at setting up churches. I don't have the answers, but I believe God would give grace, strength and wisdom to do this if we asked Him for it.

Plan your new journey

Any effort to rework old patterns and habits takes planning and a considerable amount of work. To do this one should have an idea of what to do, and how to do it. Below are a few ideas to start with.

- Rediscover the vision of the Kingdom. Define what God intended for His church…you! Remember that the church does not exist for its own self-protection and gratification. It exists to accomplish a purpose for the King. Do you know what the purpose is? Is the purpose simply to exist and remain existing, or is it to live and accomplish something? What is the church supposed to accomplish? Jesus left us four things He wanted us to accomplish in Mt 28: 19 & 20:
-
    - Go
    - Make Disciples.
    - Baptize them.
    - Teach them to obey His commandments.

Where Do We Go From Here?

- Chart the things the church needs to accomplish for the Lord. Be specific. **This is a process**, it doesn't just happen. It's something that needs to be given thought, planning and action. It involves equipping (Eph. 4: 12, 13). Everything you do as a church needs to flow from your stated vision. In other words, your stated vision needs to be and remain your functional vision. (The stated vision is what you say, the functional vision is what you do.) It is nice to say you want to follow the Great Commission, but how are you going to do this? The rest of what you define for yourselves needs to agree with this vision and implement it. Much has been written about this by others. The important thing to recognize is that everything a church does reflects how they view their vision, regardless of whether or not the vision is written. They demonstrate their functional vision by what they actually do and the priorities they make for themselves.

- Understand and define your leadership model. This includes understanding what servant leadership means to you, how it relates to the vision, the brotherhood, and the Lord.

- Understand the need for, the purpose of, and the types of standards and their effects on the church.

- Extract, define and apply the biblical standards already given in Scripture. Most Anabaptist church standards contain, without realizing it, both cultural standards and Biblical standards. Learn to recognize the cultural ones and eliminate them. They usually come in the form of defining colors, sizes, lengths, styles, features, materials, technology levels, etc.

- Develop a joy and appreciation for discipleship and companionship (a love for the brethren). This means cultivating a zeal and interest for togetherness as a brotherhood.

➤ Establish regular times of assembly beyond regular worship times.

➤ Develop a Gospel centered plan of involvement in the society around you.

➤ Develop and implement a plan for equipping the church (brotherhood) for the work of ministry. This involves a variety of things. Church is not about programs and ministry offices. It is about taking the four things Jesus asked the church to do and making sure you have a means of accomplishing them. How are you going to take a new acquaintance and carry them through the process of turning them into a disciple, baptizing them and teaching them how to be a disciple? How will you make sure someone knows what being a Christian is supposed to look like? What are you relying on to communicate the essentials of Christian life to the new person? How does a new family learn to know the others in the church? How are they going to be brought to a point of being a functioning part of the body? How will they be able to understand and become committed to your church vision? All of these things are a process. You need to define those processes, and make sure they are communicated well to everyone, and that everyone understands them and remains committed to them.

Examples of Church Functions

Jesus vision for His Church involves process, *doing*. This process involves Going, Making, Baptizing and Teaching disciples. You could probably come up with other similar terms. The process is not complicated nor intended only for professionals or specially gifted people. We are all appointed to do this. It is our duty as believers. But we don't have to do this alone. Jesus intended for all of us in the local body to be a part of this process. For an example of this idea, see *Simple Church*, by Thom S. Rainer and Eric Geiger.[11]

Going

People are not born knowing how to reach out to those around them. They need to learn how to do this. This does not come without work. Plan to equip everyone with deliberate teaching and training for the work. Jesus gave us the commission for this work.

Witness

"*...and you shall be witnesses to Me in Jerusalem, and in Judea and Samaria, and to the end of the earth.*" (Acts 1:8).

- Witness to the brethren and sisters in the church through love. (Jerusalem).
- Witness to those who have a profession of faith. (Judea) Most of America claims to be Christian. But our responsibility is to live a lifestyle consistent with the Christianity we profess. Living by biblical standards, and being able to communicate with the surrounding society is vital.
- Witness to those who have an awareness of God, but are uncommitted. (Samaria). We currently tend to shy away from associations with such people. We want to remain isolated from them unless they come to us. Maybe it's appropriate to find ways to go to them in a non-confrontational, loving way.
- Witness to the rest of society. (The uttermost parts of the earth.) This type of outreach could mean much loss to us in this life. It may mean leaving our comfortable homes and society and going to

---

[11] Rainer, Thom, and Eric Geiger. 2006. *Simple Church*. Nashville, TN: Broadman & Holman Publishers.

uncomfortable places. Where will the Lord take us? Am I willing?
- Being ready to give an answer to everyone for the hope that you have.
- Being prepared to send and be sent.
- Invoking the Spirit's guidance and power.

How could this work be done? A common way we have done this is by planting new church bodies. This is biblical, and is more of a long term method. It can take a great deal of resources, depending on how you define the Church. Does it need a large facility? Does the church require large farms or big shops? Does a church need complicated and expensive programs? All these should point back to the vision. What does your vision require? This could be a large topic to discuss, but I will leave it for now. What other ways can you think of?

Urbanize
The Plain People have made it almost a cultural mandate to settle in rural areas. This fits well with other parts of the culture. But in the beginning it was not so. Many Churches were located in cities. What about us? How can we do this? Should we plant churches in cities? Why not? Is Anabaptism exclusively a rural religion? Consider sending two or more mature brethren to areas for short or long term outreach. They should be equipped to start bible studies, disciple those responding, and perhaps be ready to help them start a church in that area. This would take serious work and dedication by the church for this endeavor. It would not be a sideline.

Innovate
A church motivated for this purpose could be very effective in developing methods of outreach when not

hindered by cultural expectations. It is important to remember that success is not measured by numbers of responses. An effort does not necessarily mean trying to reach large numbers. The kingdom is built one soul at a time.

Making Disciples

Like outreach, God gave us gifts to be used for turning men into disciples. Once a person responds to your presentation of the Gospel, then what? A disciple does not just happen once they respond to God's call. Disciples are made. They need to be brought to a point of maturity. With the power of the Holy Spirit, the Church makes them.

How are they made? As an illustration, consider the one who develops symptoms of some health problem. Suppose he has severe pain and other symptoms he can't understand. He decides to go to the emergency room, and get some help. How does it go from there? Is he required to find his way through the hospital, locating the diagnostic equipment and the people to run them? Does he wander the halls looking for the right department to develop a treatment plan? I think you get the point. He is taken step by step through the diagnostic and treatment process. I emphasize the word *process*. It is a process to take him from being sick to being well. He does not know the process, nor the particular steps to take. The steps to take for him may be different for each person who comes to the ER. But the equipment and personnel are the same.

The analogy holds for the Church. Each person who steps into the Church needs to receive the same type of care and direction. The church needs to know the steps and direction to take for each soul in its care. He is your responsibility and in your care. You need to know how to take him from a position of unbelief to a position of entering eternity. One point of caution I would add would be aware of the temptation to rely on the Sunday worship time to fulfil that need. But that is not the purpose of Sunday worship time. The Sunday worship sermons should be used to direct everyone to various aspects of the Worship of God, and the encouragement of the saints to a closeness to God. There simply is not enough time available in the Sunday morning time slot to accomplish what is needed to make disciples. That requires a separate dedicated time and effort.

Baptizing Disciples

Jesus specified baptism as one of the important things in the building of His kingdom. Each of his subjects needs to be baptized into his Body. His disciples are to be the ones to do the baptizing. Do they know how? Are they familiar with the importance of this step? Can they communicate the meaning and reasons to the new believer, so that they have the convictions and commitment needed to endure to the end? I don't need to develop this here. That's not the focus of this writing. Others have done this better than I can. But it is important to recognize the place this fits into the process the Church develops to fulfill Jesus' command.

Teaching Disciples

Remember how Paul complimented the Roman believers in their ability to teach? *"And I myself also am persuaded of you, my brethren, that ye also are full of goodness, filled with all knowledge, able also to admonish one another."* (Rom 15:14) The word translated *admonish* also means teach. He said that Jesus *"gave some to be apostles, some prophets, some evangelists, and some pastors and teachers, for the equipping of the saints for the work of ministry..."* (Eph. 4:11-12). Of course, Paul was one of these. I believe he motivated their desire (they were full of goodness). He gave them the knowledge (filled with all knowledge). He enabled them (gave them the ability). In other words, he discipled them. Paul continued in Eph 4:12 *"for the edifying of the body of Christ."*

So did Jesus ordain men to be consultants and experts for the body to come to in times of need? I don't believe so. I think they were sent to equip the body to minister to the body. This equipping involves time and effort to train men and women to do this type of work. No one was born with this knowledge. It is acquired. It will either come from within or without the body. The leadership is responsible to see that the saints are given tools needed for the mission.

Establishing

A new believer needs to have a foundation of faith established. They need to be taught to obey Jesus commandments, and how to do so. For young people, this is the responsibility of the parents. But even the parents may need help. Do the parents know how to disciple and what to explain? Whether it is the parents or others, who will do this? Do they know how? Everyone needs to be equipped to equip.

Restoring

Despite the best discipleship efforts, we all will fall some time. The church should know how to restore such a person. This is not simple or trivial. It is an area most neglected in Plain churches today. Much could be said about this. Rather than relying on counseling centers or Psychiatrists, the church should equip itself to help the people with besetting sins, or the married couples with relational problems. This involves more training, and that can be obtained from many sources. This needs serious attention, and great care. Like alternative medicine, counseling can cover quite a broad spectrum of beliefs and approaches. But, only those methods recognizing that true healing comes only from Jesus Christ, and only through a cleansed heart free of idols should be considered. For an overview of this approach, see "*Solomon's Guide To Worship Disorders.*"[12]

Small Groups

Jesus started the first small group ministry when he selected his 12 disciples. Small groups - even in a small church - are important for implementing and maintaining principle based standards. Everyone needs to know one another well enough to rebuke, exhort, admonish and edify. The standards (i.e. principles) form the skeleton for a sound body, and caring interaction gives it flesh and life. (Ez 37:1-10)

I found these thoughts by Mark Shaw expressing this well:

> *"We have too many "sitters and soakers" who make excuses for not making disciples when there are no acceptable excuses, because this is a command of Christ. Paul and Barnabas obeyed the command to go, and they then made more disciples of all nations. The disciples they made were disciple-makers who produced disciple-makers who produced disciple-makers, and so on. The world has never been the same. Today, the church must reclaim the relational element of making disciples and caring for souls. Pulpit ministry is a good start, but it is not enough. Paul ministered the Word both publicly and privately. (Acts 20:20). Many churches are strong in the pulpit (public proclamation of the Word) yet struggle in the private (one to one, or house to house) proclamation of the Word. Members do not know how to live out the Word in their personal lives, marriages, and families. They hear a solid*

---

[12] Johnson, Thomas C., *Solomon's Guide To Worship Disorders*, Smyrna, ME, Solomon's Press, 2016.

sermon each week ... but the intimate 'iron sharpening iron' area of disciple-making is too often non-existent. In family life, crisis marital situations abound as a result.

Our culture desperately needs men and women who are discipled to stand through the trials of life to reflect the glory of God in a fallen, sin-cursed world. Followers of Christ need the preaching of the Word, small group fellowships within the faith family centered upon the Word and prayer, and the personal ministry of intimate disciple-making centered upon the Word and prayer. These are not optional areas for the believer today." [13]

One Anothering

With over 50 references in the New Testament referring to "one another" we should have a good idea how to relate to each other. This involves casual interaction, as well as intentional meetings. The more effort a church invests in equipping its people for the work of ministry, the stronger it is and the greater its strength to resist the temptations of this world. The strength of a church comes through its members and their relationships, not through its fences.

---

[13] Mark Shaw, ***Paul The Counselor***, Focus Publishing, 12

No Greater Burden

Summary

We need to recognize the goal. The goal is to be the Bride of Christ; in the world and not of it. It means seeing the difference between that and a religious ethnic society. If we can see that, the work can begin. Then we can rethink and redesign our church around the original New Testament pattern of worship and service. It's important to see that a Church exists to make disciples. This is a process, and must not be left up to the individual to figure out how to get himself discipled. The process needs to be clear, simple and part of the vision of the Church. Each church would need to approach this with prayer, brotherhood interaction and work to rebuild on a new foundation of disciple making.

The sun has set and time is late. I'm tired. I hope you have been able to follow my train of thought and can have a bit of sympathy for an old seeker who is still seeking. I appreciate what I have been given, and want nothing more than to be content with where I am. But I also need to remember the fact that, as one sister put it, we should never be content this side of heaven.

There is much work to do. I would really like to continue sitting on my front porch and watching the view. This is a figurative way to say that I would like to remain in my comfortable, secluded, protected church setting. But I continue to sense that the situation is serious. I need to get busy.

Conclusion

Conclusion

Let's pull this all together...

The temptation to want everyone to look and act alike is strong, it's human and natural. It feels comfortable. But, the Bible does not define these specific things for us, nor does it allow us to require them. We feel we must, though, in order to be unified. So we...

- ❖ Make applications of principles.
- ❖ Protect them with sanctions.
- ❖ This forms a culture.
- ❖ This develops into an ethnic society.
- ❖ The society preserves itself for generations.
- ❖ Undesirable traits creep in.
- ❖ Kingdom vision erodes.
- ❖ Spiritual life suffers.

The result of this process is that our culture gives us the appearance of close brotherhood while endangering that closeness. It gives the appearance of being the Kingdom, with an eroding Kingdom vision. It is a distraction, almost a numbing force, because we tend to rely on it to do for us what we should do by God's help. It reduces the need to really know each other, because we reason that if we are dressed right and hold to the prescribed standards, we are spiritually well. Unity of spirit has morphed into uniformity of practice. The Kingdom vision of making disciples has morphed into a vision of cultural preservation, at the expense of spiritual vitality. This type of society can be duplicated without spiritual involvement and the presence of it is not proof of it being a spiritual entity.

> *"There is a peculiar change that takes place when you begin to think less about yourself and pursue oneness in the body of Christ. Instead of the members of the church*

becoming the same, they become more unique. **Oneness is not sameness.**"[1]

Is it wrong then, for a group to agree on how they should look and function? In other words, is it wrong to produce a culture? I believe that people are given that choice. Any group of people can come together with ideals and goals. It doesn't seem to be wrong to me to discover areas of similar understanding, and stick together because of those similarities. But how long will those areas of agreement last? What does the group do when the similarities change? If the group came together voluntarily in the beginning, how can the voluntary nature of the group continue? Can the original nature of the group preserve the original agreements and still retain the voluntary nature of the group? This, I believe, depends on what binds the group together. In other words, upon what is the unity based?

People will change. It seems understandable to want to preserve a sense of agreement. It follows then to create understandings which bind the group together, and maintain the original look and feel. But, the moment the group relies on those understandings to keep them together, it is only a matter of time until that unity is lost. This was clearly demonstrated in the breakup of the Christian Communities.

The most serious problems occur, however, when Christian groups establish their own sets of applications based on what they think are Biblical principles, and then use *those applications* as the basis of uniformity. The temptation then follows to teach those newly formed agreements as Biblical doctrine. Teaching adherence to the group's cultural agreements as a Biblical requirement and using social sanctions to enforce agreement is where the chief error lies. It connects the culture of the group to relationship with God. It makes

---

[1] Edward T. Welch, ***When People Are Big and God is Small***, Phillipsburg, NJ, P&R Publishing, 1997, (215)

Conclusion

use of the strong family ties within the group as an unstated lever to require acceptance of the agreements. It uses the fear of losing relationships with family and God in order to maintain the culture. This spawns many progressive problems as time goes on, as we saw in Part I and II. I see this as a chief candidate for being sin, since Jesus did not seem to authorize such a use of Biblical sanctions. People become less important than the culture. The Christian church is not a natural thing, but a living, spiritual thing.

I acknowledge that diminishing the importance of culture by returning to unity of principle does not mean the elimination of problems. It creates new ones. But the problems it may create are addressed in the charter of the upside down kingdom Jesus created. They were anticipated and addressed in the principles and instructions He gave us. Through the working of the Holy Spirit within a properly functioning brotherhood of believers, these problems can be addressed. But, problems created by man-made innovations are more difficult to deal with.

The desire to create a safe and comfortable society is natural, not spiritual. ***But this results in burdens that neither our forefathers nor we are able to bear.***

What do you think? I encourage you to dig into your Bible and other resources and see what you find. Look carefully, with no assumptions.

> *"For a remedy to this dilemma there is only one place to go. There is no physical solution, for it is not a physical problem. The problem is spiritual. There must be a return to the Word of God by all ministers, parents and any others who care...Don't do as hundreds have done in the last fifty years. They gave up and let it ride. The church has gone backward tremendously since the time of early America. The Anabaptist vision is almost totally lost. The church will*

go into complete apostasy unless people wake up and return to the Word of God. We dare not rely upon tradition to save us. We must be persistent. The church must be brought back to God. The big problem is most likely a fault of the system rather than any particular individual. If we start to fuss about whose fault it is we will only create more problems. We need to begin cleaning up without wasting any time on blaming people." [2]

Now I will go to bed, and pray that God will give you and I clear direction. Good night, and remember…

> **Unity of principles,
> strong brotherhood,
> and servant leadership
> results in
> Kingdom Christianity**

> **Unity of applications
> results in
> an ethnic society
> with weakened brotherhood,
> loss of Kingdom vision
> and hierarchical leadership**

---

[2] Stephen L. Yoder, *My Beloved Brethren*, 1992, (164)

Epilogue

Epilogue

In the year and a half that has passed since beginning this study, our lives have changed significantly. Part of our family has joined the ranks of those seekers who, as I described in Part I, didn't *make it* in the Old Order setting. It would be reasonable and expected for you to ask why. But I suspect that you could have detected some hint of this during your reading of this work. If you are like many, you could have been asking yourself, "How can they continue to be a part of a setting like that with the type of questions they are asking?" Indeed, those questions don't suggest an outlook that is in total agreement with that way of life, and that way of thinking. So, the inevitable happened. Our balance scale tipped past center. We realized that we did not fit any longer. The decision and time came to move out.

It was a hard task to include some of my thinking from 20 years ago in this writing. I was very tempted to scrub out some of the assessments I made of my life back then, the goals I had, and the decisions I made. But I hope it will be helpful to others to see how it went for us and what we were thinking. Maybe others can identify with it. I should make it clear at this point, though, that we don't regret the path we took. We did the best we could with what we knew. Life is a journey. This portion of our journey has brought us blessings in many ways. But it was not without pain.

I also debated whether to critique what I included in the Introduction. I thought about remarking about how different some of those things look to me now. But I think it is best left unsaid, at least in print. If you have questions, feel free to contact me.

I do not think it is possible to examine a separation like this in an unbiased way. No matter who looks at it, there will be preconceived ideas, presumptions, expectations, emotions and experiences that drive the questions and the answers. I feel there is no point in trying to find fault. Over the years, I have watched people come and go. Generally, their leaving resulted in poor feelings between the parties. The ones who left blamed the church, and the church blamed the ones leaving.

If I have any hope of any benefit to come to others as a result of our experience, it is in three areas:

1) That the church we left and others like it may continue to serve the Lord in a way that allows them the courage to take a peek at what has been discussed here. I hope to provoke a consideration of things that make up Christ's commission, and what may be a hindrance to them.

2) That others who may be considering a move *into* such a setting would consider it carefully. It's important to consider as many angles as possible. I've not thought of all the angles, but may have added a few to the list. Friends, be sure this is what you want to do before committing to it. It's too hard on

Epilogue

the people you join, and yourself to jump in and then out again.

3) That no one can say we are blaming anyone for what we did. Since we are the ones who chose to join, and the ones who chose to leave, we are the ones who are responsible for what we did and the decisions we made. No one else is. Most importantly, I am hoping to show that it is not a problem with the people per se, but the culture under which they have been raised. It is a layer above them. It is a hard layer between Christ and his church. That layer is the problem in my opinion.

Now we press on as members of another form of Anabaptist church. As is often said, it is not a perfect church, and if it were, it would no longer be with us as members. We strive to do our part in our new setting. Please pray that we will.

All Glory To God.

Thomas C. Johnson

Plain City, Ohio

2018

Article XIX

# Appendix 1 - Article XIX

Below is Article XIX of the *"Confession of Faith According to the Holy Word of God"*, written around 1600 AD. This can be found in the Martyrs Mirror.

Signs of the Church of God

Of the signs of the church of God, by which it may be distinguished from all other peoples, we confess the following:

First – Saving Faith
In the first place, all true Christians are known by the only saving faith, which works by love. It is wrought, through the grace of God, in the heart of man by the hearing of the Word of God, and hence, is not founded and built upon human decrees, but upon the Word of God alone; and it works so effectually that by it we are drawn and impelled from all visible things and sinful lusts of this world to the invisible God and His heavenly riches.

Second – New Birth

Secondly. All true children of God are known by the second or new birth, from above, of God; which is wrought by the Spirit of God internally in the heart, through the putting off of the sinful lusts of the flesh; so that, as man, through his first birth of the flesh, brings forth his human nature and mind; so, through regeneration, he becomes a partaker of the divine nature, by which he is also to bring forth godly and spiritual fruits, and the mind of Christ Jesus.

Third – Good Works

Thirdly. The church, or the believers, are known by the good works which they evince as fruits of gratitude from their faith; which may not be done according to human instructions, in a self-selected holiness, but in which we follow Christ and His apostles, as they prescribed and walked. And with these divine virtues all true believers must be clothed, that, as a light on the candlestick, and a city on a hill, they may excel and shine among all men, and may be known thereby, as a good tree is known and distinguished by its good fruits.

Fourth – Purity of Heart

Fourthly. The church of God is known by the glorious appellations by which she is described and honored by the Holy Spirit, as a city and temple of the living God, in which God will dwell and walk; the bride of the Lamb, the daughter of Zion; a chaste virgin, joined to Christ by faith; so that, even as with all cities which are subject to the command of their Lord and king, and it may thereby properly be known, under whose power and dominion they belong, so also the church of God is known by this that she recognizes and obeys Christ Jesus as her only Head and King, in all matters of faith, and observes His commandments. And as a pure virgin and bride forsakes father, mother, and all strange company and subjects herself to the will and obedience of her only bridegroom; so all true children of God must separate themselves from all false worship, flee from the stranger's voice, and unite themselves to Christ, to hear and obediently follow His voice, which is proclaimed by the ministers sent by Him.

Fifth – Faithful Ministers

Fifthly. The people of God are known by their faithful ministers, who, according to the doctrine of Paul, are unblamable in doctrine and life, and feed the sheep of Christ, not for the milk and wool, but with a willing mind, with knowledge and understanding; speaking not their own words, but only the words of their Lord, and executing His work; rightly dividing and dispensing the Word of God, and bringing forth fruits with it; in order that through this good message of the ways of the Lord men might, according to the counsel and will of God, be converted from their evil ways, and won to God.

Sixth – Godly Love

Sixthly, and lastly. All true disciples of Jesus Christ are known by the unfeigned godly love, which our Savior Himself has put as a sign, by which His disciples should be specially known; which is comprehended in these things: That we love the Lord God our Creator with all our heart and strength, above all other things, which consists principally in the keeping of His commandments. And besides: That we love our brethren or neighbors as ourselves, not only in word or tongue, but indeed and in truth; so that those to whom God has given spiritual gifts, minister therewith, from love, to the souls of their neighbors; and those whom God has blessed with temporal possessions, minister therewith unto the temporal needs of their neighbors, in order that thus among this true Israel of God, there may be found no poor, nor any lack in spiritual or temporal things.

Demonstrating Christianity to the World

Finally, we must show charity to all men, though they be our open enemies, who persecute and kill us, whom we may by no means resist with carnal weapons; but, as Christ did not open His mouth in revenge upon His enemies, but, as a humble and dumb lamb, prayed for them, so we must also follow this infallible example. And as all soldiers forsake their former avocation, and wear the livery of their lord and king, as a sign to distinguish them from all strange servants, and that they are bound to their captain even unto death; so also, must all true servants of Jesus Christ be armed with the aforesaid marks, that thereby they may be known and distinguished from all other people. Where, therefore, men believe with the heart, in the Father, the Son, and the Holy Ghost, and in the incarnation, justification or redemption, suffering, death, resurrection, and ascension of Jesus Christ, and the resurrection of the dead and the eternal judgment; and where, besides, the ordinances of the Lord, as baptism, Supper, separation, and the like, are rightly observed, according to Scripture, and Christ is followed therein, in the clean fear of the Lord, and in the regeneration there is the city and church of the living God, the pillar and firm ground of the truth, the tabernacle of God with men, in which God will dwell and walk with His Spirit. Such a body [church] has Christ for its Head, Preserver, and Savior. But where said marks do not exist, and where the ordinances of men are the rule of action, there is no church of God, but a vain boasting of the same.

How the true faith is to be known, read, "So then faith cometh by hearing, and hearing by the word of God." (Rom. 10:17), "He that believeth on me, as the scripture bath said, out of his belly shall flow rivers of living water." (John 7:28), "That your faith should not stand in the wisdom of men, but in the power of God." (I Cor. 2:5), "For in Jesus Christ neither circumcision availeth anything, nor uncircumcision; but faith which worketh by love." (Gal. 5:6) See also Heb. 11:1; Hab. 2:4; Heb. 10:38; Rom. 1:17.

How the children of God are to be known by regeneration or the new birth, read, "Being born again, not of corruptible seed, but of incorruptible, by the word of God, which liveth and abideth forever." I Pet. 1:23, "Jesus said unto them, Verily I say unto you, that ye which have followed me, in the regeneration when the Son of man shall sit in the throne of his glory, ye also shall sit upon twelve thrones,

Appendix 1

judging the twelve tribes of Israel." Matt. 19:28, "For in Christ Jesus neither circumcision availeth anything, nor uncircumcision, but a new creature." Gal. 6:15; John 3:8; II Cor. 5:17.

How the true members of Christ are. To be known from their godly conversation, read, "Every tree that bringeth not forth good fruit is hewn down, and cast into the fire. Wherefore by their fruits ye shall know them. Not everyone that with unto me, Lord, Lord, shall enter into the kingdom of heaven; but he that doeth the will of my Father which is in heaven." Matt. 7:19-21; 5:16; 12:50; john 15:1; Sir. 19:24, "Do all things without murmuring and disputings: that ye may be blameless and harmless, the sons of God, without rebuke, in the midst of a crooked and perverse nation, among whom ye shine as lights in the world; holding forth the word of life." Phil. 2:14-16., "Little children, let no man deceive you: he that doeth righteousness is righteous, even as he is righteous. He that committeth sin is of the devil." I John 3:7, 8.

How the people of God are to be known from this that they have separated themselves from all other people, and put themselves under Christ their Head, hearing only His voice, and observing His commandments, read, "Wherefore, my dearly beloved, flee from idolatry. Ye cannot drink the cup of the Lord, and the cup of devils: ye cannot be partakers of the Lord's Table, and of the table of devils." I Cor. 10:14, 21, "Be ye not unequally yoked together with unbelievers: for what fellowship hath righteousness with unrighteousness? And what communion hath light with darkness? Wherefore come out from among them, and be ye separate saith the Lord, and touch not the unclean thing." II Cor. 6:14, 17; Rev. 18:4; Isa. 52:11; Jer. 15:19; 51:6, "As I said unto you, My sheep hear my voice, and I know them, and they follow me. And a stranger will they not follow, but will flee from him; for they know not the voice of strangers." John 10:26, 27, 5, "Teaching them to observe all things whatsoever I have commanded you." Matt. 28:20; II Thess. 2:15; John 8:31; 14:21; 15:10; Matt. 11:28; I John 3:7.

No Greater Burden

How the false prophets are to be known and distinguished from the true servants of Jesus Christ, read, "Beware of false prophets, which come to you in sheep's clothing, but inwardly they are ravening wolves. Ye shall know them by their fruits." Matt. 7:15, 16; Dent. 13:1, "He that speaketh of himself seeketh his own glory: but he that seeketh his glory that sent him, the same is true, and no unrighteousness is in him." John 7:18, "For he whom God hath sent speaketh the words of God." John 3:34; 8:31; I Pet. 4:11, "But if they had stood in my counsel, and had caused my people to hear my words, then they should have turned them from their evil way, and from the evil of their doings." Jer. 23:22, 31; Isa. 55:11; Matt. 23 throughout; Col. 1:6; read also Tit. 1:6; I Tim. 3 throughout.

How Christians are to be known by their love, read, "*A new commandment I give unto you, that ye love one another; as I have loved you, that ye also love one another. By this shall all men know that ye are My disciples, if ye have love one to another.*" John 13:34, 35; I John 3:23, "*In this the children of God are manifest, and the children of the devil: whosoever doeth not righteousness is not of God, neither he that loveth not his brother.*" I John 3:10; 15:12; Matt. 22:39; Eph. 5:2; I Pet. 1:22; II Pet. 1:7.

No Greater Burden

NO Greater Burden

The Servant Leader

Appendix 2 - The Servant Leader

The likelihood that a church would be able to function as Christ intended is in part based on the leaders. This is a high calling. It cannot be performed effectively in the flesh. It requires the anointing of the Spirit of God. Servant leaders follow the pattern of Christ in their leadership. Below are a few of their characteristics.

Serves a High Calling

- ❖ Has clear vision for the direction to go.
- ❖ Knows the process needed to accomplish the vision.
- ❖ Communicates and inspires the vision in his people.

Appendix 2

Committed to His People

- Equips, motivates, trains, and activates his people.
- Knows the strengths and gifts of his people.
- Is committed to their good over other things.
- Serves his people by enabling them to use their strengths and gifts.
- People are more important than the organization.
- Sees himself at the bottom, seeing to the effective working of his people above him.

Expects Much

- Has high expectations for his people.
- Trusts his people.
- Holds his people accountable to their own abilities and convictions.
- Has confidence in and builds the confidence of his people.
- Underperformance brings coaching and encouragement, not rejection.
- Does not need to micro-manage.

Blazes a Trail

- Moves ahead to see where to go and prepares the way for his people.
- Anticipates, seeks to find and works to remove problems and barriers that hinder his people.
- Gives clear direction in the process needed to accomplish the vision.

Builds On Strengths

- ❖ Knows his people well enough to know their strengths.
- ❖ Enhances their strengths.
- ❖ Matches strengths with the vision.
- ❖ Plugs his people into the <u>process</u> needed to accomplish the vision.
- ❖ Helps them be fulfilled in their place.
- ❖ Delegates responsibilities.
- ❖ Looks for problems and removes them so his people can accomplish the vision.

Effective Communicator

- ❖ Knows how to communicate his ideas to others.
- ❖ Is interested in listening to his people.
- ❖ Expects and equips communication between his people.

Resourceful In Meetings

- ❖ Has a clear agenda for each meeting.
- ❖ Encourages participation, draws out ideas and incorporates them.
- ❖ Encourages brainstorming and innovation.
- ❖ Does not dictate.
- ❖ Draws conclusions.
- ❖ Formulates plans from results of the meeting.
- ❖ Confirms common understanding of decisions and direction with the others.
- ❖ Makes sure everyone knows who needs to do what.

No Greater Burden

No Greater Burden

Bibliography

Anonymous. AD 160. "Epistle To Diognetus." In *Ante-Nicene Fathers Vol 1*, 70. Hendrickson Publishers.

Geiser, Bryce. 2000. *A Closing Chapter For The Christian Communities.* Old Order Notes.

Hoover, Peter. 2008. *The Secret of the Strength.* Primitive Christianity Publishers.

Hostetler, John A. 1993. *Amish Society.* The Johns Hopkins University Press.

Johnson, Thomas C. 2016. *Solomon's Guide To Worship Disorders.* Smyrna, ME: Solomon's Press.

Kuruvilla, Finny. 2013. *King Jesus Claims His Church.* Anchor Cross Publishing.

Martin, Andrew C. 2007. *Creating a Timeless Tradition, The Effects of Fundamentalism on the Conservative Mennonite Movement.* Waterloo, Ontario, Canada: Thesis.

Martin, Donald. 2013. *Joy In Submission.* Wallenstein, Ontario, Canada: Vineyard Publications.

Peck, M. Scott. 1983. *People of the Lie.* New York, NY: Simon & Schuster.

Publishers, Pathway. 2016. "Understanding Depression." *Family Life*, August - September.

Rainer, Thom, and Eric Geiger. 2006. *Simple Church.* Nashville, TN: Broadman & Holman Publishers.

Schaff, Philip. 1858. *History Of The Christian Church, Vol 2.* Hendrickson Publishers.

Schlabach, Theron F. 1988. *Peace, Faith, Nation.*

Shaw, Mark. n.d. *Paul The Counselor.* Bemidji, MN: Focus Publishing.

Tripp, Paul David. 2002. *Instruments In The Redeemers Hands.* Philipsburg, NJ: P&R Publishing.

van Bracht, Thieleman J. 1660. *Martyrs Mirror.* Herald Press.

Verduin, Leonard. n.d. *Anatomy Of A Hybrid.* The Christian Hymnary Publishers.

—. n.d. *Reformers and Their Stepchildren.* Christian Hymnary Publishers.

Welch, Edward T. 1997. *When People are Big and God is Small.* Phillipsburg, NJ: P&R Publications.